D0523047

Kronion. Hitherto, the prevailing opinion has been that the Doric temple was built in 650 B.C., and was originally small, with only a "pronaos", and that it was extended in 600 B.C., when it acquired an "opisthodomos" and a pteron. Recent research suggests, however, that the temple may have been built in a single phase and with a unified plan in 600 B.C. The Heraion, which is long and narrow and has heavy proportions, is one of the earliest examples of monumental temple construction in Greece. The lower part of the temple, which is preserved along with the enormous orthostates of the cella, is made of the local shelly-limestone, while the upper part of the walls were of unbaked bricks, and the entablature of wood, with terracotta tiles on the roof. The apex of each of the pediments was adorned with a clay disc-shaped "akroterion". The columns were originally made of wood, being gradually replaced by stone ones over a period of some centuries. Each column was replaced by another, one in the style of the period in question, so that the columns reflect the complete development of the Doric column, and especially the capital, from the Archaic period to Roman times. Inside the cella is preserved the base on which the stone statues of Zeus and Hera stood. The colossal head of a goddess (Λ1) found during the excavations belongs very probably to this statue of Hera (fig. p. 79).

Treasuries

Shortly after this, the *treasuries* began to be built; these were small temples in the shape of the "megaron", and were dedicated by the Greek cities, mainly of the colonies. They were erected on the natural terrace on the southern slopes of Kronion, a little higher than the Heraion. The earliest treasury (that of Sikyon in its first phase) is almost contemporary with the Heraion, while the latest (those of Sikyon and Gela in their second phase, and those of Syracuse and Byzantium) date from the first half of the 5th century B.C. They stood in a row, one next to the other, and formed the northern limit of the Altis. Though Pausanias mentions the names of ten treasuries, the ruins of twelve small temples survive in this area; however, only five can be identified with certainty – those of Sikyon, Selinous, Metapontion, Megara and Gela. Originally, these treasuries probably served a cult purpose, but later were used to house valuable votives.

Pelopion

The *Pelopion* (the shrine of Pelops) was remodelled in the 6th century B.C. The wall enclosing it, which had originally been circular, now became pentagonal, and a propylon was built, which was replaced by a more monumental one in the 5th century B.C. It has recently been suggested that the Pelopion dates from the 4th century

*a) The Heraion from the east. To the right, a part
of the Nymphaion and in the background the columns
of the Palaistra.*

*b) The Zanes to the left and the Krypte, the passageway leading to
the Stadium.*

*c) The Stadium from the west. On the northern embankment,
the altar of Demeter and on the southern one the exedra
of the Hellanodikai. The starting line is at the beginning
of the race course.*

a

b

c

B.C., but this view does not seem to be well-founded.

Prytaneion   At the beginning of the 5th century B.C. the *Prytaneion* was built in the north-west corner of the Altis. This was the headquarters of the "prytaneis", who were officials of the sanctuary. There was a special room for the sacred hearth, with its eternal flame and official guests and victors in the Games were entertained in the northern part of this building.

Great Altar of Zeus   The *Great Altar of Zeus* stood to the south-east of the temple of Hera, but no trace of it has been preserved. It gradually acquired the shape of a mound from the ashes left from the sacrifices and the hearth of the Prytaneion, but this was washed away by the rains after the sanctuary ceased to function. The area in front of the Altar, especially the slope near the terrace on which the treasuries were built, was probably the "theatre" referred to by Xenophon. It received its name from the view (= θέα) it offered of the area where sacrifices were made and other rituals enacted.

Stadium   The Archaic *stadium* (Stadium I), which was simple in form and had no proper embankments, probably ran along the terrace of the treasuries. Its narrow western end, where the finishing line was, lay open and faced the Great Altar of Zeus. Stadium II, which took shape during the end of the 6th or the beginning of the 5th century B.C., assumed roughly the same position, possibly slightly further to the east; the track was on a lower level, how-

ever, and the longer sides now had regular embankments. Towards the middle of the 5th century B.C. the stadium (Stadium III) was again moved, 82 m. to the east and 7 m. to the north, and its narrow western side closed in. Recent excavations have shown that the embankment of this western side was truncated after the mid-4th century B.C., to make room for the *Stoa of Echo*, which separated the stadium completely from the sanctuary. Until this period, the stadium had been included within the sacred area, since the games had a purely religious significance. Now in its final position, cut off from the sanctuary, it changed in both form and character. (Recent excavations indicate that Stadium III can be dated to the early 5th century B.C. and Stadium II to the Archaic period).

From that time, the Games, too, began to change their nature, and gradually became merely a spectacle for entertainment. The track in this new stadium is 212.54 m. long, and ca. 28.50 m. wide, while the starting and finishing lines are 192.28 m. apart, as opposed to the 186 m. of the Classical stadium. The embankments surrounding the stadium on all four sides did not have stone seats. Apart from a very few stone seats reserved for important persons, such as the "exedra" for the "Hellanodikai", on the south embankment of the stadium, opposite the *Altar of Demeter Chamyne*, the 45.000 spectators that the stadium could hold sat on the ground.

During the Hellenistic period (latter part of the 3rd

Reconstruction of the Hippodrome. To the left the starting post
(Drawing : K. Iliakis).

century B.C.), the north-west corner was connected to the sanctuary by the *Krypte,* a narrow, vaulted corridor that had a gate with Corinthian columns at the west end.

Krypte

On the site of this post-classical stadium, excavations revealed numerous springs which had already been tapped in archaic times to secure sufficient water for the thousands of visitors who attended the Games. When the stadium was moved there in the 5th century B.C., they were filled in; during the recent excavations they were found to contain many offerings dating from the Geometric, Archaic and Classical periods, many of them of exceptional artistic merit.

Hippodrome

The *Hippodrome,* which had a total length of four stades (ca. 780 m.), has not been excavated, and it is probable that at least part of it has been washed away by the Alpheios. It acquired its final form and position, to the south of and parallel with the stadium, during the Classical period. It was then that a new means of operating the starting mechanism of the horse and chariot races was introduced. A small elevation in the ground to the north of the course of the hippodrome was converted into a regular sloping embankment for the spectators, and artificial embankments were created to the south and west by dumping soil there. The western limit of the hippodrome was the Stoa of Agnaptos, which remains undiscovered.

The course in the hippodrome was elliptical and was divided along its axis by a stone or wooden partition two stades long (ca. 390 m.). The riders and charioteers turned both ends of this partition, which separated the course into two parts, so that it covered a total distance of 4 stades, or ca. 780 m., on each circuit.

Bouleuterion

Finally, the southernmost of the two *Bouleuterion* buildings in the southern part of the sanctuary was constructed after the middle of the 6th century B.C. of rectangular shape, with one of its short sides in apsidal form, it was a continuation of the types of prehistoric building found in the Altis. During the 5th century B.C. the second, also apsidal, building was added parallel to the first, while between the two of them was erected a square building containing the *Altar of Zeus Horkios,* on which the athletes swore the oath required before the Games. These three adjoining buildings were connected, possibly during the 4th century, by an Ionic stoa along the eastern side.

The sanctuary reached the height of its wealth and prosperity in the 5th century. It was then that the most important building in the Altis was erected – the great *Temple of Zeus.* Construction of it commenced in ca. 470

Temple of Zeus

B.C., immediately after the reorganisation of the state, and was completed in 456 B.C. This Doric peripteral temple was the work of the Elean architect Libon. The largest in the Peloponnese, it was considered the perfect expression, or "canon" of the Doric temple. The marble sculptures on the pediments depicted the chariot race between Oinomaos and Pelops, with Zeus in the middle, on the east side, and on the west, the battle between the Lapiths and the Centaurs during the wedding of Peirithous and Deidameia, with Apollo in the middle. The twelve metopes, six above the entrance to the "pronaos", and six above that of the "opisthodomos", portrayed the twelve labours of Herakles. These sculptures, now partially restored and displayed in the Olympia Museum, are the most representative examples of Greek art of the "Severe style". The central "akroterion", of the east pediment was a gilded Nike (Victory), the work of Paionios. The same artist who sculpted the marble *Nike* which stood on the high triangular pedestal in front of the east facade of the temple of Zeus. The side "akroteria" were gilt "lebetes". A chryselephantine statue of Zeus seated on a throne, sculpted by Pheidias, was set up inside the cella in about 430 B.C. This magnificent work is described in detail by Pausanias, but only inferior reproduction of it survives, mainly on Elean coins. The gigantic figure of the god held a Nike —also made of gold and ivory— in his right hand and his sceptre in his left. The throne and base of the statue were decorated with mythical scenes featuring gods, daemons and heroes, in gold, ebony and precious stones.

A special *Atelier* was built to the west of the temple for working on the statue. Large numbers of tools, glass ornaments, clay moulds and other objects connected with its production have been found in and around the atelier, and make it possible to assign a definite date to the statue of Zeus.

Two other buildings were erected to the north of the workshop at about the same period. One of them, which is rectangular and has a peristyle court, is usually identified with the *Theokoleon,* which housed the "Theokoloi", the priests of Olympia. The other, to the west of the Theokoleon, is a circle inscribed in a square in plan; according to the late Hellenistic inscription found in the area this is the *Heroon*. Recently it has been proposed that it originally housed the baths and was only later dedicated to an anonymous hero, but there is no firm evidence for this.

Still further west towards the Kladeos, lay several *baths* and a *swimming-pool*, also built during the 5th century.

a) Reconstruction of the east side of the temple of Zeus with pediment. →

b) Reconstruction of the west side of the temple of Zeus with pediment. →

c) Reconstruction of the interior of the temple of Zeus with the chryselephantine statue of the god. →

Nike of Paionios

Pheidias' Atelier

Theokoleon

Heroon

Baths

a   c

b

The temple of Zeus. View of the cella from the west.

*The Metroon. View from the west. To the left, part of the stepped
retaining wall of the Treasuries.*

Around 300 B.C., the baths were extended, as they were again in 100 B.C., when they were fitted with hypocausts. These baths were abandoned in the Roman period, when hot baths were built in many parts of the sanctuary.

The late Classical period saw Elis troubled by both internal discord and clashes with its neighbours. However, these difficulties did not prevent new building activity, which gave the sanctuary its final form and architectural appearance. It was then that the delicate Ionic and Corinthian styles were introduced into Olympia, where previously the dominant form had been the austere Doric, with its heavy proportions. Much use was made of white marble in the new buildings, replacing the shelly-limestone that had been used almost exclusively up to that time. This was symbolic of the general change in the character of the sanctuary that was also apparent in the Games held there. During this period the stadium was relocated to the east of the Classical stadium, completing its isolation from the Altis.

Stoa of Echo

This separation became total, as we have seen, with the construction of the *Stoa of Echo* along the east side of the Altis. This stoa was also called *Heptaëchos,* because sounds re-echoed seven times in it. It was also known as *Poikile* (painted) because of the frescoes decorating its interior. Built shortly after 350 B.C., it had two colonnades, the outer Doric, and the inner possibly Corinthian, with rooms at the far end.

In this period, the sanctuary proper was segregated from the ancillary and secular buildings by a monumental "peribolos" of poros, with five gates, three in the west side and two in the south.

Metroon

The *Metroon,* the temple of Cybele, Mother of the Gods, was built at the beginning of the 4th century B.C. in front of the terrace of the treasuries. A Doric peripteral temple, only the stylobate and parts of the stone entablature have survived. The Metroon was used for the cults of the Roman emperors from the period of Augustus, and many statues were set up in it. The bases of 16 bronze statues of Zeus, the *Zanes,* erected with the money from the fines levied on any participants found guilty of cheating in the Games, still stand along the terrace of the treasuries, between the Metroon and the stadium.

South Stoa

The *South Stoa* formed the southern boundary of the sanctuary. This had two colonnades, the outer Doric and the inner Corinthian, with a wall behind it. Its facade, which faced the Alpheios, had a projection on columns in the middle of it, making the stoa T-shaped. It was built at about the same time as the Stoa of Echo, and like it, had a base and steps of marble.

The *Southeast building*, belonging to the 4th century B.C., lay to the south-east of the stoa. An altar to Artemis was recently discovered near the south-east corner of the Hellenistic extension of this building. The latter was demolished in the 1st century A.D. so that a peristyle villa, probably that of Nero, could be built on its foundations.

The *Philippeion*, the circular peripteral building south of the Prytaneion, was begun by Philip II after the battle of Chaironeia (338 B.C.), and was completed by his son, Alexander the Great. It rested on a marble stepped crepidoma, most of which is preserved, and had a row of Ionic columns around it. Corinthian half-columns, divided the inside wall of the circular cella and at the far end, opposite the door, five statues, representing Alexander the Great, placed between his parents and forefathers, stood on a semicircular pedestal. The statues, made of gold and ivory, were the work of Leochares. This circular type of building, which was traditionally of religious character, was now used for the first time for mortals in the cult of the Macedonian dynasty, who were considered by some to be semi-divine.

The guest house, the *Leonidaion*, was erected about 330 B.C., in the western part of the sanctuary, south of the workshop of Pheidias. It is named after its architect, Leonidas of Naxos, who also furnished the finances for it. All four sides had rooms, which faced inwards into a peristyle court with Doric columns while an Ionic colonnade surrounded the outside of the building. Initially intended for official guests and distinguished visitors, the Leonidaion was converted in the Roman period into a dwelling for Roman officials.

No new buildings were erected in the sanctuary proper during the Hellenistic period (3rd-1st centuries B.C.). The only work undertaken was that of preservation and repair, and occasionally of extension of the old buildings, though sometimes this was on a large scale, due to the damage caused by frequent severe earthquakes. However, building activity continued in the area outside the Altis, where comfortable quarters were designed for both athletes and visitors.

To the west of the Altis, near the Kladeos, in an area long used for training the athletes, the *Palaistra* (wrestling-school) was built in the 3rd century B.C., for practice in wrestling, boxing and jumping. It was roughly square in shape (66.35 × 66.75 m.), with a peristyle court, surrounded by covered areas sectioned off into special rooms for undressing, anointing the body with oil, powdering it with dust, bathing, as well as rooms with benches for lessons in theory.

a

a) *The eastern part of the Gymnasion with the Palaistra in the background.*

b) *The byzantine Basilica with the double inner colonnade and the panel of the iconostasis.*

b

Gymnasion

To the north of the palaistra and adjoining it was the *Gymnasion,* a closed rectangular building (120 × 220 m.) with a spacious court in the centre, and stoas on all four sides. This was where the athletes trained for events that required a lot of space, such as the javelin, discus and running. It was built in the early 2nd century B.C., though its monumental entrance, in the form of an amphiprostyle Corinthian propylon, probably belongs to the end of the 2nd century B.C.

The picture of Olympia is completed by the thousands of altars and statues of gods, daemons and heroes, as well as of Olympic victors, kings and generals, all of them works of the most famous artists of antiquity. Very few of these have survived, and in many cases we have only the bases. Similar works were erected during the Roman period, most of them statues of Roman officials and emperors; these were set up not by the individuals concerned, but by cities or private citizens who wished to secure their favour. The most valuable of the earlier works were at this time transferred to the Heraion, which assumed the character of a museum.

In 146 B.C., the Roman consul Mummius, having crushed the Greeks at the Isthmus, dedicated 21 gilt shields at Olympia, which were affixed to 21 metopes of the temple of Zeus. By contrast, Sulla, in 85 B.C., plundered the treasures of the sanctuary, as he did those of Epidauros and Delphi, to obtain the finances needed for his war against Mithridates. Sulla even decided to transfer the Olympic Games to Rome, and the 175th Olympiad was held there in 80 B.C. Olympia only recovered from the decline that began at this date after 31 B.C., during the reign of Augustus. Roman emperors and official continued to show their interest in the sanctuary and the Games in a variety of ways, as part of their political programme for Greece. Under Nero, the Altis was extended and a new peribolos constructed, 3 m. beyond the old enclosure on the west side and 20 m. beyond it on the south, and the simple gateways of the sanctuary were replaced by monumental entrances.

Hot baths

At the same period, *hot baths* were built to the west of the Greek baths, and also to the north of the Prytaneion. Later on, still more were added, to the north-east of the villa of Nero, and to the west of the Bouleuterion. A new guest house was constructed to the west of the workshop of Pheidias. During this period the earlier buildings were restored or converted.

Nymphaion

Finally, Herodes Atticus built his aqueduct in A.D. 160, channeling the waters of a copious spring, 4 kilometres east of Olympia, into the imposing *Nymphaion,* or *Exedra.*

This was semicircular in shape and had two small circular temples in front of it, one on each side; the walls were made of baked brick faced with coloured marble. Statues stood in the niches on the face of the semicircular, probably two-storey wall. These depicted Antonious Pius and his family, and the family of Herodes Atticus. Between the two small circular temples, two cisterns were placed at two different levels, one in front of the semicircular wall and one lower down. The water ran into the higher, semicircular cistern and from there into the lower, rectangular one, from where it was channeled to the whole of the sanctuary by a vast network of conduits.

The first serious destruction of the monuments of Olympia took place in A.D. 267, when a wall was constructed in great haste to protect the valuable treasures, and particularly the chryselephantine statue of Zeus, from the threat of the Herulians, who, in the end, did not get as far as the sanctuary. The wall, formerly thought to be Byzantine, enclosed the temple of Zeus and the south part of the sanctuary as far as the south stoa. It was built with material from the other buildings both within and without the sanctuary, which were demolished for the purpose, the only exception being the temple of Hera. The sanctuary survived for a further century in this truncated form, and in an ever increasing state of decay, though some building repairs took place, mainly under Diocletian (A.D. 285-305). Its life came to an end in A.D. 393 with the decree of Theodosius I forbidding the functioning of heathen sanctuaries. There followed the demolition of the Altis in A.D. 426, as a result of a decree by Theodosius II, and two major earthquakes completed its destruction in 522 and 551 A.D..

In the 5th and 6th centuries A.D. a small settlement of Christians established itself at Olympia, and the workshop of Pheidias, the only building still standing, was converted into a *Christian basilica*. Subsequent flooding of the Alpheios and the Kladeos, together with the erosion of Kronion, whose sandy soil had become denuded of trees in the meantime, finally covered the whole sanctuary with a deposit of silt 7 m. thick. The Kladeos, furthermore, changed its course, washing away many of the buildings in the west of the sanctuary.

The first efforts to discover the monuments of Olympia were those of the French "Expédition scientifique de Morée", in 1829. Systematic excavation in the sanctuary was begun by the German Archaeological Institute in 1875, and has continued to the present day.

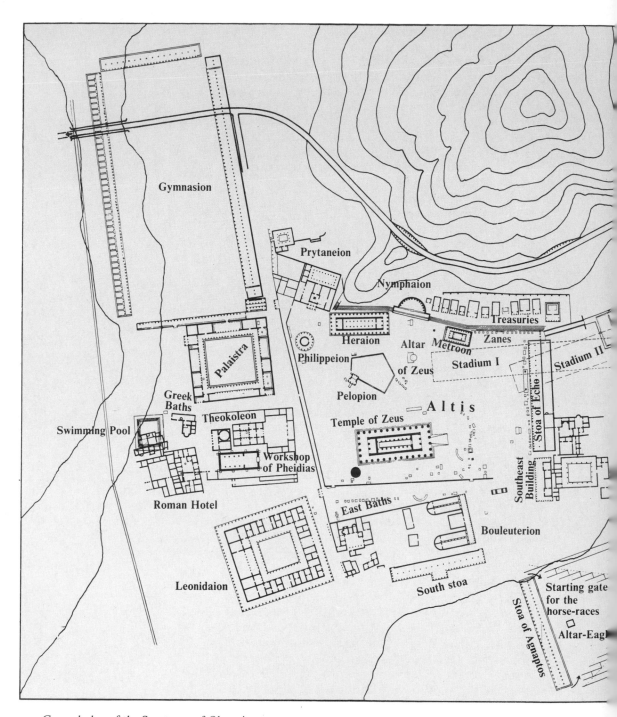

General plan of the Sanctuary of Olympia.

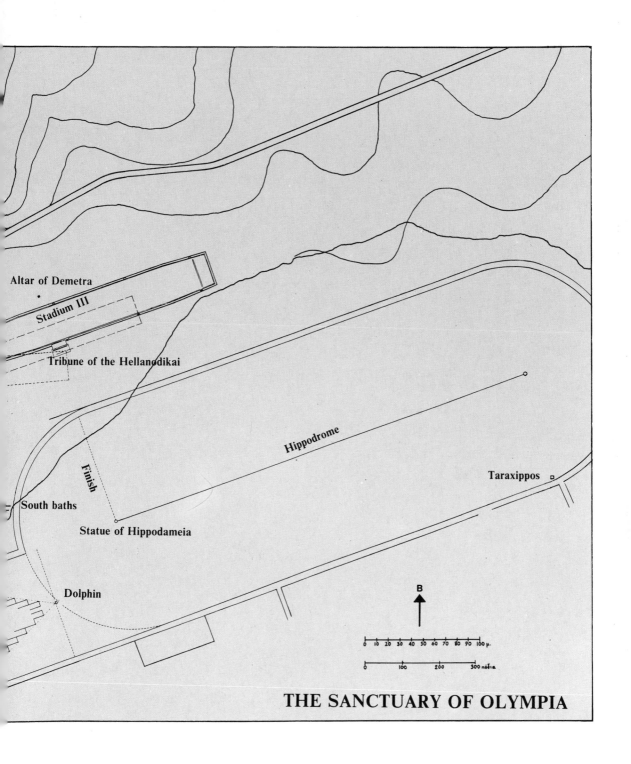

Altar of Demetra

Stadium III

Tribune of the Hellanodikai

Finish

Hippodrome

Taraxippos

South baths

Statue of Hippodameia

Dolphin

B

0 10 20 30 40 50 60 70 80 90 100 μ.

0   100   200   300 πόδια

THE SANCTUARY OF OLYMPIA

Reconstruction of the monuments of the Sanctuary of Olympia
(by A. Mallwitz). →

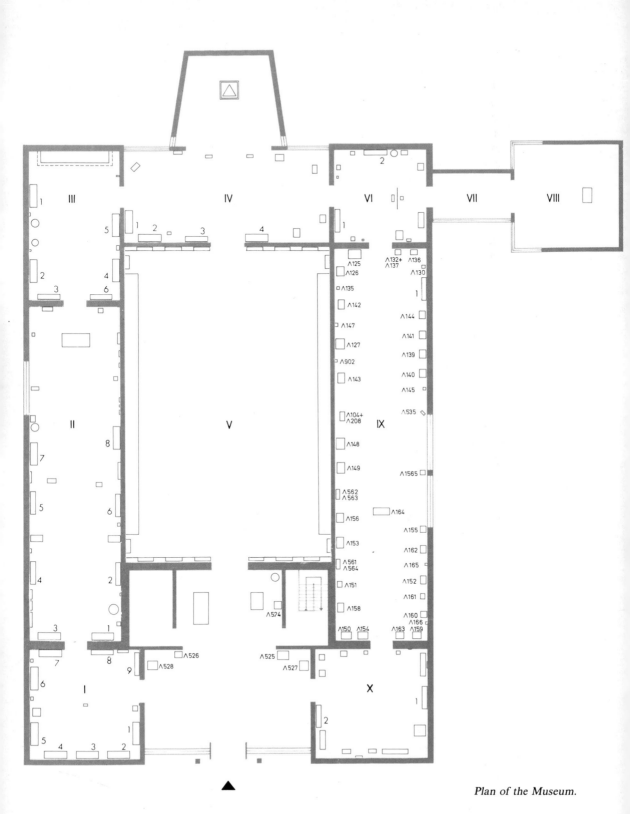

Plan of the Museum.

THE MUSEUM

The first museum at Olympia was erected in 1888. It was a handsome neo-classical building on a hill west of the Altis. The building, known as the Syngreion, was named after the well-known Greek benefactor Andreas Syngros, who donated the money for its construction. However, as time passed and finds from the excavations multiplied, the building became increasingly incapable of performing its functions satisfactorily. After the damage it sustained in the earthquakes of 1954, the restoration work and underpinning required merely aggravated its inadequacies. A new building was therefore planned, to occupy a site in a valley northwest of the hill of Kronos. It was finished in 1975 but not officially inaugurated until 1982, after all the exhibits had been re-arranged.

Among the many priceless works on view, the most impressive are the sculptures from the Temple of Zeus, the Nike of Paionios (or Paeonios) and the Hermes of Praxiteles. Although few marble sculptures from the Hellenic period have been found in the Altis, there is no dearth of examples from Roman times.

What the sanctuary held in even greater abundance were bronze votive offerings – statues, figurines, tripods, weapons, armour, and so forth. Naturally, only a few fragments have survived from the large statues of gods and athletes cast in bronze – a material exceptionally well suited to the rendering of the "sun-tanned athlete" and the contests in which young men excelled. But the minor art works in the Museum make up the richest collection of this kind in the world.

Pottery is also well represented at Olympia. Vases – for the most part undecorated and intended for everyday use – figurines and ornamental building components, such as sima, water, spouts, pedimental statues and acroteria, abound. Most of them adorned archaic buildings made of shelly limestone or porolithos; The collection of terracotta architectural ornaments is one of the finest in existence.

Over all, the exhibits reflect the brilliance and magnificence of the most renowned panhellenic sanctuary of antiquity and constitute an impressive encapsulated history of Greek art, spanning over a thousand years, making the Museum of Olympia one of the most important in Greece.

ENTRANCE HALL

Plan of the Entrance Hall.

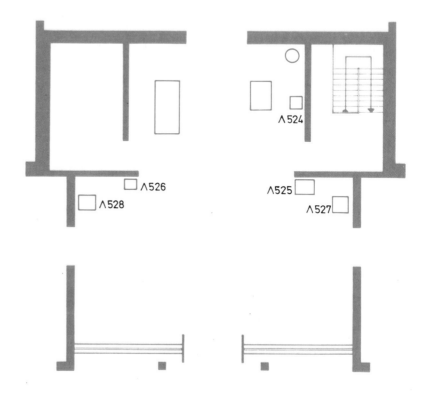

Λ527. Base of the statue of the boxer Euthymos of Epizephyrian Lokroi, in Pentelic marble. The statue, which does not survive, was executed by Pythagoras of Samos and was erected after the athlete had been victorious in the ring in three successive Olympiads, those of 484, 476 and 472 B.C. On the front of the base is the inscription: *Euthymos of Lokroi, son of Astykles, won three times at Olympia. He set up this figure to be admired by mortals. Euthymos of Epizephyrian Lokroi dedicated it, Pythagoras of Samos made it.*

It seems, however, that this is not the original inscription but a restoration with some slight changes introduced to make it look as though Euthymos himself was the person who had erected the statue. It may in fact have been donated by somebody else, possibly by the city of Lokroi.

Λ525. Marble base for the votive offering of Mikythos. Mikythos was the slave of Anaxilas, tyrant of Rhegium (494-476 B.C.) and came to Greece when he was banished from Rhegium in 467 B.C. The inscription on the front has been reconstructed to read: *Mikythos, son of Choiros from Rhegion and Messene, inhabitant of Tegea, dedicated these statues to all the gods and goddesses. After spending all his money on doctors to cure his son who suffers from a consumptive disease, he came to Olympia to pray for help. ...os dedicated it.*

Pausania, who mentions Mikythos' many offerings, noted that *"he dedicated the offerings at Olympia in fulfillment of a vow made for the recovery of a son who was ill with debilitating disease"*. Another similar inscription, has also been found.

Λ524. Black limestome pedestal for the statue of the great sophist, Gorgias of Leontinoi, erected by his sister's grandson, Eumolpos, in the fourth century B.C. to honour him as a friend and teacher. The inscription, on the front of the pedestal, reads: *Gorgias of Leontinoi son of Charmantides. Deicrates was married to the sister of Gorgias; she begot him a son, Hippocrates. Hippocrates' son, Eumolpos, dedicated this statue as a tribute to his education and friendship with Gorgias. Until now, no mortal has discovered any art better than Gorgias' for training the spirit for contests of Virtue. A statue of Gorgias has also been dedicated in the valley of Apollo* (at Delphi), *as an example not of wealth but of piety.*

Λ526. Base for the statue of the boxer Kyniskos from Mantinea, made in Peloponnesian marble. The inscription, preserved on the upper rim, reads: *Kyniskos, the boy boxer named after his father, from the famed city of Mantinea, dedicated it* [this statue].

Pausanias says that Polykleitos made the statue of Kyniskos, the child boxer from Mantinea. To judge by the style of the letters, which cannot be later than the middle of the fifth century B.C., it almost certainly was a work by Polykleitos the Elder.

Λ528. Base of the statue of the pancratiast Callias of Athens, made of Pentelic marble. Round the top read the inscriptions: *Callias, son of Didymios the Athenian* [victorious] *in the pancration. Micon the Athenian made this.* Micon is better known as a painter; according to Pausanias, Calllas was victorious in the seventy-seventh Olympiad, 472 B.C.

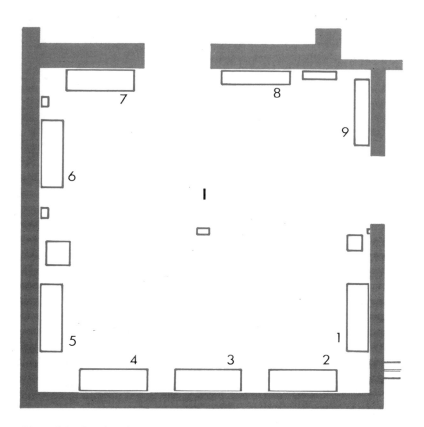

Plan of the Prehistoric-Geometric Hall.

PREHISTORIC - GEOMETRIC GALLERY

This gallery houses an exhibition of finds from the Early Helladic (E.H.), Middle Helladic (M.H.) and Late Helladic (L.H.) eras, the Cycladic and also the Geometric periods.

The *Early Helladic Period* (approximately 2800-2000 B.C.) is represented by only a few examples of pottery: vessels of the type known as "sauce-boats" and large pithoi with applied relief decoration.

The *Middle Helladic Period* (approximately 2000-1600 B.C.), in contrast to the Early Helladic period, is represented by a significant quantity of pottery and other objects which came from the dwellings in the Altis. There are two typical groups of pottery, the Minyan and the Matt. The former, sometimes but not always wheel-made, is monochrome, in varying shades of grey and has a smooth, almost glossy surface. It was produced in a variety of shapes; most were wine cups (skyphoi) with tall ribbon-like handles or cups with a long horizontally fluted stem.

K1220. Kantharos of the "Minyan" type.

The matt ware, bowls or several variants of pithoi, was usually hand-made. The decoration, in black, white or red covering the upper part of the vessel, was initially of rectilinear patterns, later replaced by curvilinear designs.

A third category here is made up of vessels with incised decoration. Though they were produced locally, they share many features with pottery from other Middle Helladic settlements in Greece.

Case 1

The vessels **K1242** and **K1279** (bottom shelf), known as "sauce-boats" together with some others of the same type such as **Π2971** and **K1213** (top shelf) and fragments of large pithoi, date from the EH period; they are the oldest

K1206. Oinochoe with incised decoration.

37

Π2511. Terracotta figurine of the Ψ type.

Δ28. Necklace made from glass paste beads.

indication of habitation on the site. Other chance finds of the same period from the surrounding area are displayed in Case 2. The kantharoi **K1219, K1225** and **K1220** (top shelf), of the MH period and of the Minyan type came from dwellings sited in the Altis and its adjoining area. The vessels **K1204 – K1208** (middle shelf) with their beautiful patterns and carefully executed incised decoration were products of local workshops. The obsidian flakes and other stone tools are contemporary with the pottery.

Case 2

In addition to the Altis other neighbouring areas have produced finds from the EH and MH periods: the site of the New Museum and Pisa, as the German archaeologist Dörpfeld christened the hill east of Olympia at the junction of the main road to Tripoli with the road to the village of Miraka. For example, the anchor-shaped objects **Π2536 – Π2539** (middle shelf), found on the site of the New Museum, date from the Early Helladic period.

It is not certain whether the row of tools on the bottom shelf dates from neolithic times or constitute survivals of Neolithic types in the Early Helladic period.

The Late Helladic or Mycenaean Period (approximately 1600-1100 B.C.) is divided into three sub-periods: early LH I (1600-1500 B.C.), middle LH II (1500-1425 B.C.) and late LH III (1425-1100 B.C.). The third period, which lasted much longer than the preceding two, is in turn sub-divided into three main phases, which correspond roughly to the 14th, 13th and 12th centuries. The dating corresponds mainly to the development of pottery styles.

Most of the Mycenaean exhibits in the Museum come from burials. There are three kinds of Late Helladic graves: cist graves, chamber tombs and, the least common, tholos tombs. The first are simple hollows, the second subterranean chambers, which in Elis were dug into the soft sandstone hill sides. The tholos tombs were rather similar to the chamber tombs, but were built into the hillsides and covered by a beehive-shaped roof.

The most characteristic vessels of the Late Helladic period are the stirrup jars, Kylikes, alabastra, jugs, cups and little kraters. Their decoration, whether with geometric patterns or motifs taken from plant or marine life, is either zonal or covers large surfaces. Following the diffusion of Mycenaean civilisation over the entire Mediterranean basin in the 13th century and later, and the overproduction of its wares which flooded the markets, it was inevitable that quality should suffer and a standardisation of both shapes and decoration set in.

The Mycenaean tombs which have been discovered in the region of Olympia mostly contained pottery. In some, however, weapons, jewellery, seals and figurines were found. Weapons (swords, daggers, spearheads and arrow heads) and some tools (knives, razors, tweezers etc.) were of bronze.

In contrast to the Early and Middle Mycenaean objects which bore lavish decoration, the later weapons were usually plain or were ornamented only on the pommel to which ivory plaquettes or gold leaf was attached. After 1300 B.C. the older type of sword, elongated and with a mushroom-shaped crown to the pommel, was supplanted by a new type. This shorter sword with a T-shaped pommel and two projections on its lower part to protect the hand, was topped by a crescent-shaped projection.

Seals, either almond-shaped or lentoid, were cut from semi-precious stones. Decorative themes were chosen from the animal world; man in hunting scenes or sacred rituals is less commonly depicted. The art of seal engraving flourished and reached its peak in the 16th and 15th centuries. From 1400 onwards there was a tendency to simplification of the decorative themes which gradually became completely schematic.

The most beautiful and most dazzling examples of jewellery were fashioned in the first two centuries of the Mycenaean era. Precious metals and semi-precious stones were gradually more rarely employed, being finally replaced by glasspaste and faience. Beads in many shapes, both geometric and inspired from the plant and animal kingdoms (papyrus or ivy leaves, imitations of seeds, bull's heads, argonauts etc.), were used to make necklaces, bracelets and diadems.

Lastly, three categories of figurines may be distinguished; one replicates the natural human shape fairly closely; the other two resemble the letters Φ (Phi) and Ψ (Psi) and render the human body entirely schematically.

The Mycenaean finds brought to light during the most recent excavations both around Olympia and within the area of the sanctuary itself have completely changed the picture of its history. The old view, that Olympia had no Mycenaean phase and that life there started with the Dorian invasion around 1100 B.C. must be discarded. As we have seen, settlement on the site is already attested in the EH era, while the foundation of the sanctuary must be dated to at least the late Mycenaean period. Important finds in some quantity have come not only from the sanctuary of Olympia and close by, but also from the sur-

Π356. Stirrup vase.

Δ126. Helmet made from the tusks of a wild boar (restored).

39

a

b

c

d

rounding region. The number of sites which have been traced (see the map by Case 6) through notable finds show that Pisatis must at that time have been a rich area densely settled.

Case 3

The objects in Case 3 come from chamber tombs dug into the slopes of the hills to the north, east and south of the New Museum. The tombs formed a large cemetery. On the same slopes, above the tombs, was the settlement. Typical vessels are alabastra-like pots, kylikes, stirrup jars, little craters etc. Many smaller objects, such as spindle-whorls seals and glasspaste jewellery, were also found in abundance (Δ28). Of particular interest are a spear head, **M182a** and the blade of a dagger **M182b** (middle shelf) and the two terracotta Psi-figurines **Π2511** and **Π2512** (bottom shelf).

Case 4

Finds from the chamber tombs of the Mycenaean cemetery of Stravokephalo, northeast of Olympia: pottery, such as the stirrup jar **Π356** (bottom shelf). The hydria **Π329** with its stylised birds, spindle whorls, fragments of rock crystal, jewellery of semi-precious stones and glasspaste such as the diadem **Δ9** (all on the middle shelf).

Case 5

Finds from the chamber tombs of the Mycenaean cemetery of Trypes near Kladeos, north of Olympia, and from Stravokephalo. The important pots include the three-legged pyxis **Π592** (top shelf) and the amphora **Π561** (bottom shelf) with a distinctive pattern, a combination of a geometric ornament with the head of a bird, beads and spindle whorls, bone pins **Δ20** (top shelf), a spear head, **M177** and a dagger, **M178,** a Phi-shaped figurine **Π555** (middle shelf) and a restored helmet made from the tusks of a wild boar **Δ126** (top shelf).

Case 6

Vessels of various types from the tumulus of Samiko, Triphylia. The tumulus was in constant use over approximately six hundred years, for the burials date from the end of the MH to the close of the LH era. On the middle shelf, the cup **Π75** and the small jug **Π83**. Amongst the most attractive pottery is the jug **Π49** (top shelf) with its

a) *Π592. Tripod pyxis with lid.*

b) *Π561. Four-handled amphora.*

c) *Π83. Small jug.*

d) *Π49. Jug.*

Π75. Cup.

Π224. Stirrup vase.

M370, M369. Bronze spear head and dagger.

a) Π70. Rhyton.

b) Π181. Kernos.

c) Π387. Wine cup.

elegant globular shape and polychrome decoration of large stylised birds. The rhyton **Π70** (middle shelf) was intended for ritual usage. The beak-spouted jug **Π12** (bottom shelf) is particularly unusual.

It was probably in Hellenistic times that the tumulus was said to be that of the local hero, Iardanos.

Case 7

Assorted finds of the Mycenaean period from the area round Olympia (1-3) and beyond the river Alpheios (4-7).
1. From the chamber tombs close to Lakofolia (Koskina). The razor **M373,** the spearhead **M370** and the dagger **M369** are of interest amongst the bronze finds (middle shelf).
2. From the chamber tombs at Renia (Platanos) the skyphos (wine cup) **Π387** is noteworthy (bottom shelf).
3. From the chamber tomb close to Strephi (bottom shelf).
4. From Rasa and from the Alpheios dam (bottom shelf). The little krater **Π92**, of the Late Helladic II period, decorated with large ivy leaves, is of importance.
5. From the tumulus close to Profitis Ilias (Makrysia), similar to that of Samiko. The pottery spans every Mycenaean phase (top shelf).
6. From the chamber tomb at Kania (Makrysia) the stirrup jar **Π224** (top shelf).
7. From the chamber tombs of Diasela (Broumazi). The kernos **Π181** must have been a ritual vessel (middle shelf).

The *Cycladic Civilisation* (3200-2000 B.C.) produced magnificent metalwork, marble figurines and pottery.

Wall Case

The figurines in this case belong to the second phase of this culture, known as Keros-Syros. Numbers **Λ266** and **Λ267** were found at Pheia, the ancient port of Elis; **Λ265** at Neraida, Elis. They represent the best known type of Cycladic figurines, chiefly recognisable by their abstract quality, austere frontality, two dimensionality. Usually a female figure is depicted. The head is tilted backwards, the arms are folded under the breast, the knees are slightly bent and the soles obliquely turned downwards. The only sculptured facial feature was the nose; the others were rendered in paint. The significance of these figurines, most of which have been found in graves though they are not completely absent from dwellings, has been

42

a

b

c

43

B1391. Bronze figurine of a naked man with petasos (broad brimmed hat).

B1698. Bronze figurine of a naked man with helmet.

B1750. Bronze figurine of a goddess on horseback.

interpreted in many ways; one explanation is that they are images of the great goddess. Another suggests that they depict heroes or nymphs in ecstasy. Still other views hold that they are toys, or courtesans or "psychopompoi" – the conductors of souls to the underworld.

The presence of these figurines in Elis and its hinterland confirms the close network of relationships and communications that existed between the western Peloponnese and the Cyclades in such early times.

The *Geometric period* (approximately 1050-700 B.C.),- is divided into the Proto-geometric (1050-900 B.C.) and the full-fledged Geometric (900-700 B.C.) phases; the latter is subdivided into early, middle and late.

Geometric art, the first manifestation of indisputably Greek inspiration and expression, is seen to advantage in its pottery. In Olympia, examples of vases are few, but the quantity of figurines and tripod cauldrons presents a totally different and far more splendid picture, which amply demonstrates the artistic trends of the period.

On the pots, the decoration, spread across the surface in bands or registers, in a strict tectonic arrangement (a characteristic shared by the shape of the vessels themselves) is but the apotheosis of the straight line employed in endless combinations traced along a ruler – zigzags, triangles, meanders and checkers. Curvilinear decoration is also to be found, executed with a compass. Many of the same patterns also occur, in similar arrangements, in the decoration of tripods. The human form first appears on painted vases from the early eighth century. Alongside pottery, there was a sudden upsurge of development in sculpture. However, while the former had centuries of experience behind it, it was the latter which only now began to explore new means and new modes of expression. Large scale sculpture, if we except the wooden cult statues –the "Heaven sent" xoana– which have not survived, does not exist. Miniature works, in bronze and terracotta, which are abundant in the great sanctuaries and especially in Olympia, depict a variety of animals (mainly horses and bulls) and, to a lesser extent, gods or heroes. In keeping with the epic spirit of the times, man is portrayed as a charioteer or a warrior, sometimes as a dancer. The first scenes based on myths make their appearance at this time. Bronze figurines were produced in ateliers in the Peloponnese, one of the most important areas of bronze working in these early years; ateliers are known at Argos, Laconia, Elis and Corinth. Whether they were individual items or fittings for vessels such as pyxides or tripod cauldrons, the expressive abstract quality, the summary rendering of the main features and the severe articulation of the figurines seem to reflect the vision of the eternal being, man or beast. These same principles were to be venerated in the profound thought of Plato and were to be anxiously sought after in works of art.

Case 8

The exhibits in this case belong to the Geometric period; figurines of men and animals in terracotta or bronze, miniature votive tripod cauldrons and handles for large tripod cauldrons. A row of figurines at the front of the top shelf provides an illustration of their gradual evolution in the Early Geometric period. At first completely primitive and schematic, and of overwhelming simplicity, they gradually acquire flesh and therefore bulk, this achieving a uniquely expressive liveliness.

B5401. Bronze group of naked women doing a circular danse.

In the first phase, to which the figurines of men with the petasos (a broad-brimmed hat) belong, **B1391** and **B4245**, the body is naked with long legs, short arms and an ill-formed head. Facial features are not delineated; the ears and the nose protrude, but nothing else is shown.

In the second phase, represented by the helmeted charioteer **B1671**, the face is still ill-formed, as in the earlier figurines; but now, along with the ears and nose, the mouth is indicated by a deep horizontal scoring. Particular emphasis was laid on the modelling of the genitalia. These three figurines are amongst the earliest produced in the Greek world in the post-Mycenaen times.

Thereafter, attempts to render the human form became more intensive. Another figurine, **B1698**, belongs to a third phase. The various parts of the body are more naturally formed and the outline of the figure more uniform. The helmeted figurine **B24** (see Wall Case 10) belongs to an even later, more advanced phase. With the "Telchines" (**B2800** and **B3390**) (also in case 10), the history of sculpture in the Geometric period comes to an end. Steady and uninterrupted progression brought craftsmen to the breath-taking concepts which inspired the sculptures of the temple of Zeus or the Hermes of Praxiteles.

Of the remaining bronze figurines on the top shelf, the most important is the one with the raised hands, **B1391**; it depicts a suppliant mortal or perhaps a god at the moment of his "epiphany", a theme which can be traced back to prehistoric times. Some figurines of the same type (**B1698, B5377**) wear helmets. According to most scholars, they represent a god, probably Zeus, the special protector of the Doric tribes which toppled the Mycenaean

TC2285 Terracotta female figurine (Hera?).

b

c

a) Br.13261, B4350. Legs of
bronze tripod cauldrons.

b,c) B4460, Br.9694. Handles of
bronze tripod cauldrons.

d) B1671. Bronze figurines of
warriors in their chariot.

e) B24+B22. Bronze figurine of
a warrior and his horse.

46

d

e

47

supremacy. Other helmeted figures decorating the handles of cauldrons, are shown brandishing a spear in the right hand and holding a horse by the reins in the left (see **B24 + B22, B5600** in wall case 10). The theme of a goddess on a horseback, (**B1750**), the circular dance of seven naked women (nymphs;), (**B5401**), of an indisputably ritual character, also have their roots in prehistoric times. This very ancient kind of dance still survives in Greece today.

The unusually wide chariot **B1671** dates from the 9th century B.C. There is little doubt that its two occupants were two gods or epic heroes plunging into battle with zest and vigour.

Terracotta figurines found at Olympia are handmade. Though with fewer pretensions than contemporary bronzes, they too follow to a greater or lesser extend, defined types, such as the figure with outstretched arms (see **Π2949, TC8190**), the horseback riders (**Π2933**) or the charioteers. Male figures predominate, but animal figurines are also plentiful (bulls, horses etc.) (middle shelf).

Two figurines on the middle shelf are of special importance, **Π3319** and **TC2285**. The first, of the 10th century B.C., depicts a man, possibly Kronos; the second, a female figure wearing a diadem, dating from the third quarter of the eighth century B.C., is perhaps one of the earliest representations of Hera, if we are to judge from the fact that it was found in the west wing of the Heraion.

Cases 8-9 and wall case 10

Tripod cauldrons were the most magnificent and among the most numerous votive objects found at the sanctuary from the Geometric period. Whether a precious offering to the gods, or a prize in the Games –as noted by Homer– these cauldrons were a fitting oblation. In the 9th and 8th centuries, a time when works of art were being made on a small scale, they were the precursors of monumental art.

They can be separated into five groups, based on shape and technique. In the first four groups the handles and legs are cast; in the fifth they are hammered.

I. The cauldron **B1240** (next to case 5) is a typical example of the first group, which is not earlier than the end of the 9th century B.C. Its dimensions, still small, testify to its original use as a domestic vessel. The characteristically short legs, polygonal in section, and its circular handles, triangular in section, were joined to the cauldron by nailed sheets. Each leg was affixed, to the under side of the cauldron's belly with small rod-shaped brackets, so

B3390. Bronze figurine of a naked man, decorating a tripod handle.

that they stood more firmly. Both legs and handles bore rope-like decoration.

II. The cauldrons of the second group, dating from the early 8th century B.C., are more monumental than their predecessors. The handles, also larger, required additional supports at right angles to the rim of the cauldron (see **B166**, Case 8). The handles, now flat, apart from one or two protuberances, are crowned by bull's heads and later by horses. The legs are polygonal in section, the sides of the polygon being concave. The most common decoration, where there is any at all, is the spiral.

As the time passed the cauldrons became vessels with an exclusively votive use; richly ornamented and often more than one metre high.

The three last groups do not have clear chronological limits, for their dates overlap.

III. The legs at first are polygonal in section with concave sides; finally, however, they take the form of a double T. Decoration may be zigzag lines, spirals or bows etc., while on the topmost band of the legs there may be a panel with rosette, a Maltese cross or, very rarely, a scene with figures (see **B1665**, Gallery of the Olympic Games, Case 2). The handles are now perforated, with denticulated spiral decoration and are often crowned by horses, sometimes accompanied by their riders (**B24 + B22**, **B5600**, Case 10).

IV. There are few cauldrons in this group, which dates from after 750 B.C. to the end of the century. Their main characteristic is the grooves which gradually open, fan-like, towards the upper part of the legs. The handles are similarly formed, and are flat in section, crowned by horses with or without a rider. The legs continue to have double T shaped section. Scenes depicting human figures are less commonly found on the surface of the legs (see **B1730**, Wall Case left of the entrance).

V. The bronze sheets that now form the legs and handles are fastened to a wooden or iron frame. The legs retain the double T section, while the handles are completely flat. Spirals, zigzag lines and other decoration are incised on both (see **Br.9694**, case 8, bottom shelf). Because this new technique permitted the possibility of an increase in height, the cauldrons in this group can exceed two metres.

The handles, by now huge (ca. 0.30 diameter), were held in place by extra brackets which fixed the external edge of the handles to the lip of the vessel, at an angle of ninety degrees. Their lower edge is often shaped like a human hand. Later, the handles were often held in place by tall, nude supple males, balanced on the lip of the

B5700. Bronze figurine of a warrior, decorating a tripod handle.

a

b

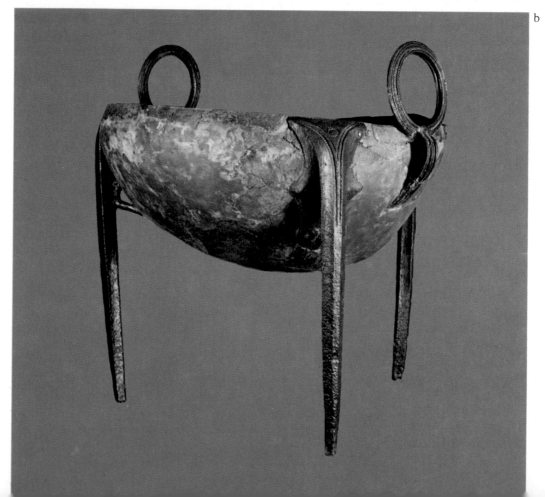

vessel to left and right, their head turned towards the viewer. According to one opinion they represent the Telchines, the mythical metalworkers (see **B2800, B3390,** Case 10). This type of cauldron, which first appears from about the third quarter of the 8th century B.C., continued in use throughout the 7th, parallel with the new type where protomes decorate the lip, as we shall see below.

To the left of **Case 1,** and between Cases **5** and **6,** stand the following tripod cauldrons and fragments of the legs of tripod cauldrons:

B1730. Upper part of the leg of a bronze tripod cauldron made in a Corinthian workshop, dating from the end of the 8th century B.C. It is not certain whether the portrayal of the two helmeted men in the upper register is meant to represent the contest between Apollo and Herakles for possession of the Delphic tripod, or simply depicts two heroes competing for the tripod which had long been a prize in the Games. On the lower register the tree of life, bordered by two confronting lions, is partly preserved.

B5229 + Br.12114. Bronze tripod cauldron, end of the 8th century B.C..

B1240. Bronze tripod cauldron, 9th century B.C. This is one of the oldest tripod cauldrons and is preserved in relatively good condition.

B1255. Leg of a bronze tripod cauldron, 750-700 B.C. It must have been immense, if we consider that its lower part has not survived.

In the centre of the gallery stands a solid bronze horse **(B1741),** dating from the transition from the Geometric to the Archaic period. It is unique for its monumental size in comparison with the small scale works of the Geometric era. The tentative, experimental efforts of the craftsman in quest of new and more impressive creations can be seen in the imperfect casting of the bronze and the poorly executed joining of the two parts which make up the animal.

a) B1741. Bronze statue of a horse.

b) B1240. Bronze tripod cauldron.

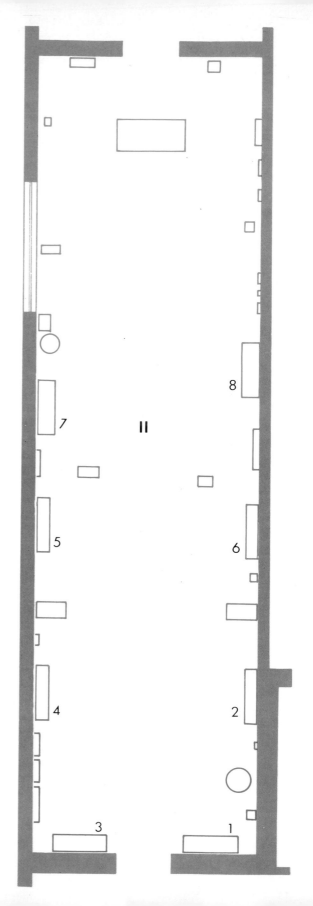

Plan of the Geometric-Archaic Hall I.

GEOMETRIC - ARCHAIC GALLERY I

Case 3

Human and animal figurines in bronze and terracotta. Some of the items in bronze decorated the handles of cauldrons of the middle and late Geometric periods. Of particular interest are the warriors **B4600** and **B2000** (Zeus?) dating from the third quarter of the 8th century and the first quarter of the 7th century respectively (top shelf), the statuettes of yoked oxen **B5618** (middle shelf), the figurines of horses **M884** and **B2377** (top shelf), the group of firugines of horses **M884** and **B2377** (top shelf), the group of figurines **Br.1106**, of dogs attacking a stag, dating from the middle of the 8th century (top shelf), and the charioteer **B1670** in his chariot (top shelf), the largest and most important of the charioteers found at Olympia, it shows a clear and robust rendering of the features (second half of the 8th century B.C.). The terracotta head **Π2954**, is of special interest.

The case also contains bronze bands with hammered or incised decoration, typical work of the Geometric period.

Wall Cases

Bronze sheets depicting gods, priests leading animals to sacrifice, riders and other themes popular in Assyrian art (**B5045, B5048, B5039, B4980, B5039a, B5047 + B5865**). Late Hittite, 8th century B.C. The sheets were reused to make a statue of a woman, while the Greek hoplites, animals and plants were unquestionably engraved by a Greek artist in the course of this reuse.

The 7th century B.C., known as the *Orientalising Period* (700-600 B.C.), was a turning point in the history of Greek art. Influences from the East had always been left in Greek art, but at this time they seem to have been overwhelming. Imaginations were stirred by tales of travel and objects brought from far-off lands which, accompanied by a greater appreciation of Nature, brought about the collapse of the Geometric canons. The artists, bored by the monotonous repetition of traditional forms and motifs and ever rootless, abandoned themselves to the enjoyment and observation of their natural surroundings,

B2000. Bronze figurine of a warrior.

a) B4600. Bronze figurine of
a warrior.

b) B5618. Bronze figurines of
yoked oxen.

c) B1670. Bronze figurine of
a charioteer in his chariot.

d) M884. Bronze figurine of
a horse.

54

b

c

d

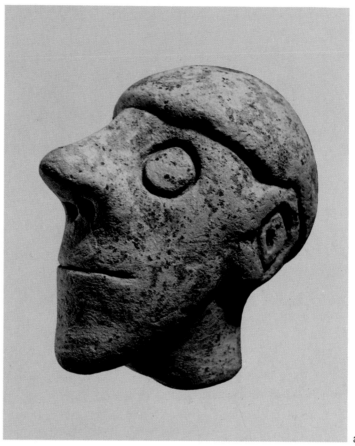

a

b

a) Π2954. Terracotta head of a man.

b) B5048. Bronze sheet with hammered decoration.

while at the same time letting their fancy roam freely in the world of legend. Works were filled with plants and flowers (lotus, palmettes, rinceaux), with creatures both wild and tame (cocks, lions) and with daemonic beings (griffins, sphinxes, winged figures). Straight lines and flat surfaces gave way to rounded shapes and full, vigourous masses. Even so, the new trends did not deflect the Greek craftsman from the principles embedded in him by his deep love for the clean-cut Geometric shapes and his instinctive rejection of every hint of exaggeration. Before the 7th century had drawn to its close, the enticing first impressions had already been subdued, and the blend of old and new was leading in fresh creative directions which were beginning to generate their own intellectual vitality. This was the century that saw the erection of the first stone temples and the emergence of large scale sculpture. At this time, too, the numerous Greek myths crystallised into their final form and were depicted on vases and on bronze sheets.

The new tendencies which came to the fore at the turn of the 8th century could not but have had some impact on the tripod cauldrons. And, indeed, at that time, a new type, based on eastern models, did develop. Protomes, most commonly of griffins but also of lions, were placed around the lip of the cauldron; at first hammered, they were later cast. Winged mythical figures were attached in the place of handles (see the cauldron **B4224**, left of the case, and the upper register of the sheet **BEIie**), while the tripod of the cauldron became a separate feature. The cone-shaped oriental base bearing hammered decoration was replaced by the tripod. Modelled figurines were affixed to the groups of rods which formed each leg, the bottom part of which was often in the shape of a lion's paw (see Archaic Gallery II, Case 2). Eventually the attachments for the cauldrons died out and so too did the lion protomes. By the mid-7th century the cauldron had acquired an established shape, its decoration confined to griffin protomes. This type was to survive into the 6th century, but as rather of the mill products; they no longer possess any special merit and merely echo the grandeur of the cauldrons of the previous century.

The older type of cauldron, however, continued to coexist alongside the newer, whose broader, longer legs opened up new creative possibilities. The scenes which now fill the broad surface of the legs are not only examples of very fine art, but are also the earliest pictorial representations of the Greek myths (see **M77**, in the small Wall Case, **B7000**, Archaic Gallery II, Wall Case to the left).

B2358. Cast bronze protome of a griffin.

57

a

b

c

d

a,b,c) Br.4312, B28, B27. Bronze handle attachments.

d) B6108. Cast bronze protome of a griffin.

Br.8767. Hammered bronze protome of a griffin.

Case 1

Representative examples of the protomes mentioned are the hammered lions **B200** and griffins **Br.8767** (top shelf). **B200**, dated 680-670 B.C., marks an important step in the development of the lion shape. **Br.8767**, with its compressed proportions, short ears and stubby korn on the forehead, is the oldest of the complete griffins, dating from 700 B.C.

The cast griffins **B2358** and **B145** (middle shelf), formerly having a hammered neck and eyes of inlaid bone, date respectively from 680-670 and 640-630 B.C. The latter is a rare example of casting, with its abominable, daemonic expression and a marvellous balance in the sharp curves which appear to be shaking as it set off by some internal palpitation.

The griffin **B6108** is of more recent date than the two preceding ones and has long ears and korn and elongated supple proportions. **B945,** dated to 630-620 B.C., has reached the final stage of development. Indeed, it is the largest example yet discovered which is cast in one piece. Both are on the bottom shelf.

Of the winged figure handle attachments, **B27** (top shelf) and **B4260**, **B4312** (bottom shelf) from the 8th century B.C.are of genuinely eastern origin, perhaps late Hittite, while **B28** and **B1690** (both on the top shelf), dating from the last quarter of the 8th century B.C., reflect their transformation at the hands of the Greeks. The dynamism and firm touch of their Greek creators contrasts with the static quality and flabbiness of the eastern prototypes.

Wall Case

Hammered griffin protome (**Br.3177**), forming part of the decoration of a monumental cauldron. This is the largest protome to have survived, and it is relatively intact. It dates from 660-650 B.C.

Of the six original protomes of lions and griffins which decorated the lips of this impressive cauldron (**B4224**), only fragments of three have survived, together with the two male winged figure handle attachments. The cauldron, with its winged figures, is late Hittite, whereas the protomes are Greek. It is dated to around 670 B.C.

Wall Case

B288. Cast bronze protome of a griffin.

Bronze sheet (**BEIie**) may have had an architectural function; for example, it may have been attached to a door or pilaster, as the holes along the edge suggest. The hammered relief work depicts, from top to bottom: a cauldron with griffin protomes on its lips, a crab, a goose and a snake (675-650 B.C.).

It is probably not just by chance that the largest collection of ancient weapons known today, mainly late Geometric and Archaic, has come from Olympia. Weapons were by far the most suitable gift to Zeus, who presided over the fortunes of the competitors in the Games at Olympia, just as he presided over the outcome of battle elsewhere. The offerings of cities from booty taken in victorious campaigns, or of individuals from their personal panoplies are not only tangible and incontestable evidence of actual historic events, thanks to the inscriptions so often engraved upon them (see for example the helmet **M9**, Early Classical and Classical Hall, in a separate case, to the left), they enlarge our knowledge of the art of war as practised by the ancient Greeks. In addition, their decoration makes a rich contribution to the depiction of myths (see the breastplates **M394**, **M397**, the belt **B4900**, Case 6), and many possess particular artistic merit (see the Illyrian helmet **B5316**, Wall Case).

B56. Bronze "Corinthian" helmet.

Case 2

Bronze "Corinthian" helmets from Peloponnesian workshops, illustrating various stages of development from the end of the 8th century to the mid-5th century B.C. It is clear that with the passing of time, their shape came to follow the contours of the skull more and more closely so that they were a better fit on the warrior's head.

Original type: **B55**, end of the 8th century B.C.

Early type: **B1499**, **B58**, **B56**, **B5615**, **B2185**; this last example has a shallow groove to accommodate the crest, a feature borrowed from the "Illyria" helmet type, and foreign to the "Corinthian" one. Beginning of the 7th century B.C. (top shelf).

Developed type (Myros group): **B1875**, **B1500**, **B7030**, **M164**, **M841a**. Mid-7th to early 6th century B.C. (middle shelf).

Late type: **B5095**, **B5085**, **B952**, **B5179**, **M9**. End of the 6th century to mid-5th century B.C. (bottom shelf).

On the wall above Case 2

Two breastplates (**B6200**, **B4744**) and two shields (**B2651** and **B1921**) (See the drawing on the wall).

B133. Winged horse hammered on
bronze sheet.

a

b

a,b) M164, B5085. Bronze
«Corinthian» helmets.

62

An inscription survives on **B2651**: (taken by) the Zancleans (as booty) from the Rhegians. It is dated to around 500 B.C. **B1921** displays its inner face and the strap by which it was held; on which were panels illustrating mythical themes, which can now only be picked out with difficulty because of heavy corrosion. It dates from the last third of the 7th century B.C.

Table Case

B110. Winged gorgoneion: hammered bronze sheet with engraved details. The eyes originally consisted of inlaid bone. The head, from which sprout ten snakes, is surrounded by a moulded chaplet with three large whirling wings. The work dates from the first half of the 6th century B.C., and is the largest shield device to have been found to date. Its diameter is between 0.90 -1.00 m. The emblem was attached to the bronze lining of the shield and, though decorative, was also intended to be "apotropaic".

B110. Winged gorgoneion, hammered on bronze sheet.

    B133. Winged horse: hammered bronze sheet with engraved details. It may have been one of a pair of similar figures, framing a plant decoration, making up a shield device, diameter approximately 0.80 m. The work, belonging to the second half of the 6th century B.C., may have come from Magna Graecia.

    Bronze and silver appliqués from the decoration of the inner side of shields.

Below the Case: Cauldron **B7650**, 6th century B.C.

Wall Case

The weapons found in the sanctuary, offerings to the god, were of exceptional quality and often richly decorated. Such, for example, is the bronze "Illyrian" helmet **B5316** with inlaid silver découpé sheets (see Case 6 for other examples of this type). On the forehead is a boar between two lions and on the cheek-pieces a horseman. The broad groove which begins on the forehead and ends a little above the flaps protecting the nape of the neck was designed to hold the crestpiece more firmly in place. It is dated to 530 B.C..

Case 6

Bronze helmets of the style known as "Illyrian", probably from a workshop in the northeast Peloponnese. They are called "Illyrian" because they were first found in the northern Balkans; their style is just a development of the

B4880. Bronze armguard.

63

a

b

c

d

Geometric type of helmet. The following stages can be distinguished: Early type: **B155**, 8th century B.C., Developed type: **B1557**, end of the 7th, beginning of the 6th century B.C., Late type: **M40**, **B5065**, mid-6th century B.C. All these are on the top shelf.

The helmet **B4667** (top shelf), dated to the last quarter of the 6th century B.C., is of particular interest, not just of its high standard of workmanship, but for its unusual cheek-pieces bearing hammered ram's heads. The helmets whose cheek-pieces are either shaped like, or decorated with, ram's heads, can be Corinthian, Chalchidean or Illyrian, such as **B4667**; they may also combine features of the Chalchidean and corinthian types, like **B4446** (Case 5, top shelf). The oldest examples of such helmets date from the third quarter of the 6th century B.C. The two conical helmets, **Br.10533**, **B51+B96** (top shelf) are made from separate sheets of bronze and belong to the Geometric period.

The same case also contains a display of offensive and defensive weapons; greaves, brassards (such as **B4880** with a gorgoneion) dating from the second half of the 6th century B.C. and possibly from Magna Graecia, the fore-armguard **B5187** (on the middle shelf), mitra for the protection of the abdomen (see also **B4900** below); ankle-guards, such as **B5010** (bottom shelf) from the first half of the 6th century B.C., probably originating from a Peloponnesian workshop, with well fashioned decoration of a sphinx and a lion's head etc; and footguards such as **B5092** (bottom shelf). Lastly, there are the tips and butts of spears.

B4900. This mitra is a splendid item from a Cretan workshop, dating from the second half of the 7th century B.C. (middle shelf). Though the subject of the decoration is difficult to identify, and could be either Menelaos threatening Helen or the murder of Clytemnestra by Orestes, the perfection of the engraving is unique, almost equalling work found in miniatures.

Wall Case

A shield **B4985** and cuirass **B5101**, of bronze. The breastplate, dating to the first half of the 6th century B.C., is unusually well preserved, the anatomical details of the chest being stressed in the modelling, though they are somewhat schematic.

Free standing Case

This marvellous breastplate, **M394**, undoubtedly be-

a,b) B5316, B5065. Bronze "Illyrian" helmets.

c) Br.10533. Bronze cone-shaped helmet.

d) B4667. Bronze "Illyrian" helmet.

B5010. Bronze ankleguard.

B5092. Bronze footguard.

a,b) B5101, M394. Bronze breastplates.

c) B4834+B4396, B1026. Bronze spearheads.

d) B4465, M907. Bronze greaves.

Br.219. Bronze spear butt with inscription.

longed to a distinguished man. Possibly the work of an island bronzesmith, it dates from about 650-625 B.C. On its lower section Zeus is depicted at the centre, together with Apollo holding his lyre. Behind Zeus are two gods, behind Apollo two goddesses, possibly the Muses or the Hyperborean Maidens who came, as their name implies, from beyond the northern regions, to Delos. The design of the plant and animal motifs which complete the decoration attest the practised hand of a craftsman with a long tradition behind him (see the drawing on the wall).

Another bronze breastplate, **M397**, of Cretan workmanship, is possibly a little older (670-660 B.C.) than **M394**. Corrosion prevents anything other than a most superficial recognition of the perfection of the hammered technique and the engraved decorative details. Between chariots and daemonic beings, the Dioskouroi are shown rescuing Helen, Theseus and Peirithous (see drawing on the wall).

Case 4

Bronze greaves; the following types can be recognised:
1. Geometric: **B7606 + B6950**.
2. Early Archaic: **B9164, B277**, end of the 7th c. B.C.
3. Developed Archaic: **M907, B2775, B2781, B2594**, first half of the 6th century B.C.
4. Late Archaic: **B450, B4465, B4995, B4462, B5756, B4743, B4202, B310**, second half of the 6th c. B.C.
5. Early Classical: **B4863, B2777**, mid-5th century B.C.

The first three groups and **B450** are on the top shelf, the last two on the middle.

Dedicatory inscriptions have been preserved on many of the greaves. On **B4465**: *The Cleonians* [dedicated this] *... to Zeus of Olympia*. On **B4462**: *The Argives dedicated this Corinthian* [booty] *to Zeus*. On **B4202**: [A booty] *offered to Zeus of Olympia*. On other greaves, such as **B4743**, the craftsman's delight and playfulness in transforming anatomical details into decorative motifs are worth noting.

Arrow heads, spear tips. **B4834 + B4396** and **B1026** and spear butts (**Br.219**) with inscription (bottom shelf)

Above Case 4: Two breastplates **B5400, B3501** (back part) and a shield **B5237**.

Wall Case

BEIie. Bronze sheet, perhaps the revetment of a larnax. On it, in hammered relief with engraved details, are two

66

a

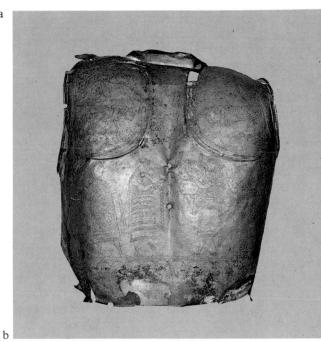

b

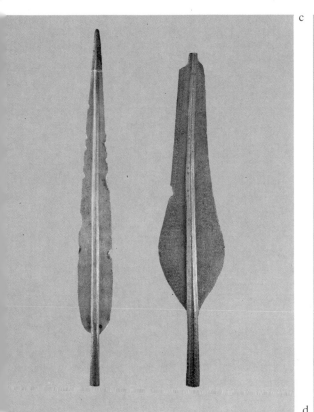

c

d

centaurs depicted in their earliest form, i.e. only their hind quarters are those of a horse. The centaurs are trying to impale down the otherwise invulnerable Kaineas, king of the Lapiths. It is an unsophisticated and refreshing product of an Ionian workshop, dating from the third quarter of the 7th century B.C. The juxtaposition of the figures, the outstanding love of detail and the decorative treatment of the trees add a lyric quality to the scene, revealing the still early Archaic spirit of this piece.

Table Case

B4990. Shield device. A daemonic figure hammered on a bronze découpé sheet, representing a winged Gorgon, with a fish's tail and lion's feet and incised details. Right down to the last detail it is a magnificent piece of work, dating from the second half of the 6th century B.C.

Appliqués from the decoration of the inside of a shield and parts of the handle. The successive panels of **B4292** depict: 1. A man leading a horse. 2. Prometheus bound and the eagle pecking at his liver. 3. Helen and the Dioskouroi.

B109. Shield device of the 6th century B.C. with a cock on a hammered découpé sheet. On the handle of the shield **B1654**, dating from the second quarter of the 6th century B.C., the successive registers portray the following subjects: 1. Lions in heraldic stance. 2. Ajax Locros and Cassandra. 3. The suicide of Ajax. 4. The murder of Agamemnon. 5. Theseus and the Minotaur. 6. Two sphinxes rampant. 7. Herakles and the lion. 8. Priam receiving the body of Hector. The only name to have been preserved from the engraved inscriptions, Adrastos, suggests that the wider register on the upper part of the handle probably bore a scene from the Theban cycle.

The entire repertory of Greek mythology is illustrated, with amazing clarity, on many of the shield handles which have been found in large quantities at Olympia.

Below the Case: Cauldron **B7590**, 6th century B.C.

Case 5

Corinthian helmet, **B2610**. Three "Chalchidean" helmets: **B5607**, **B4583** and **B4446** (upper shelf), the last one with richly engraved delicate decoration enhanced by modelling. This type of helmet, with a number of variations, first appears in the second half of the 6th century B.C. A particularly good example of the combination of "Corinthian" and "Chalchidean" features is **B4376** with mo-

a) BEIia. Bronze sheet with hammered figurative decoration.

b) B4990. Winged daemonic figure, hammered on bronze sheet. Shield device.

M130. Bronze forearmguard.

a) *Drawing of an ancient greek warrior with his defensive armour.*

b) *B2610. Bronze "Corinthian" helmet.*

c) *B4376. Bronze "Chalcidean-Corinthian" helmet.*

d) *B9097. Bronze thighpiece.*

e) *B4800. Bronze frontlet for a horse.*

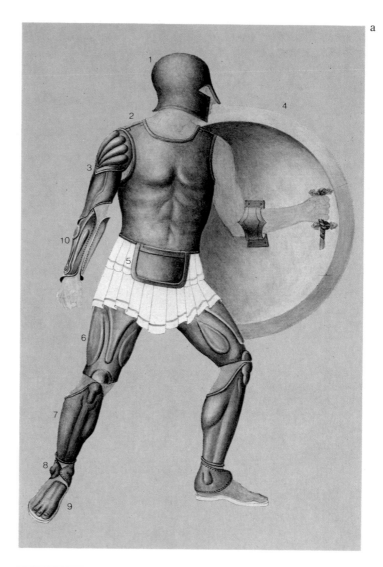

RECONSTRUCTION OF HOPLITE ARMOR OF THE ARCHAIC PERIOD

1. Helmet	6. Thigh piece
2. Breast plate	7. Greave
3. Armguard	8. Ankleguard
4. Shield	9. Footguard
5. Belt	10. Forearmguard

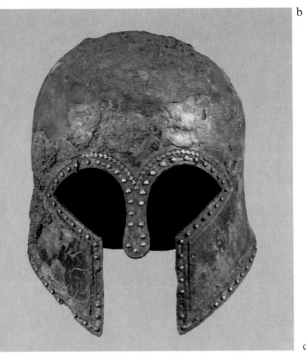

b

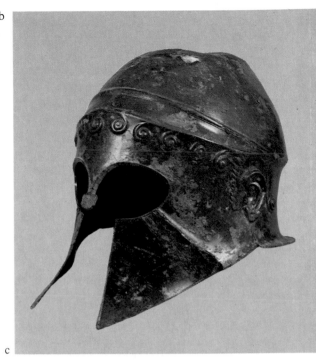

c

d

e

a

b

delled curls and ears; it comes from Magna Graecia, around 500 B.C.

On the middle shelf are pieces of armour: a forearm-guard **M130**, brassards **M41, M42**, stomach bands (mitrae), a thigh piece **Br.9097** and the faceguard for a horse (a chamfron), **B4800** (top shelf). They may have belonged to a hoard of booty from the second half of the 6th century B.C. which was offered at Olympia by some colony in Magna Graecia. The drawing on the wall shows the accoutrements of a warrior.

Wall Case

B104. A female griffin suckling her young, from a Corinthian workshop around 630-620 B.C. (see also the drawing). The figure is hammered on a bronze découpé sheet and the details have been engraved. The eye was of inlaid bone. The cub, weak and defenceless, is just visible beneath the belly of its fearsome-looking mother. This monumental work, unique in both subject and execution, indicates how Greek thought reworked a foreign concept and made it its own. In Greek art the stiff, standardised imaginary monsters and austere daemonic figures of the East, such as griffins, acquire an immediacy pulsating with the spell of nature permeating the artist. The holes in the border show that this sheet was fixed on something, but its exact use remains unknown.

Free-standing Case

B6500. Winged female daemonic figure. It is not known whether this was a single protome or if it was part of a statue. The eyes are of inlaid bone; one wing is missing. Apparently it had no arms. It is one of the very rare examples of hammered works in the round, and is thus highly valued. This example is beautiful work of 590-580 B.C. Statues were at first built up from hammered sheets hung on a wooden core. However, from the middle of the 6th century B.C. the technique of cire-perdue casting was preferred and perfected, though the protomes of cauldrons show that it was known as early as the first half of the 7th century (see **B200** and **Br.8767**, Case 1).

Case 7

Various animals from the decoration of cauldrons. Among the other objects on display the most important are:
1. The Palladium, **B4500**, one of the oldest examples of

a) B104. Female griffin with her young, hammered on a bronze sheet.

b) B6500. Hammered bronze winged figure of a woman.

D4500. Bronze statuette of Athena.

its type, 675-650 B.C. Possibly the work of a Peloponnesian craftsman, it could equally well represent Athena, Aphrodite or Artemis.

2. The goddess **B3400** wearing a beautifully decorated peplos remains unidentified since neither the head nor the symbols she would have carried have survived. It is dated to about 600 B.C.

3. The horse **B10344 + Br.2127** with the delicately worked engraved details dates from the first half of the 7th century B.C.

4. The warriors **B1999**, **B1701**, from the second quarter of the 7th century B.C. came from a workshop in Elis. In both examples, the long survival of a Geometric type is clear (See **B24**, Prehistoric-Geometric Gallery, Wall Case). The taut healthy flesh still follows the rigid Geometric tradition, just as the conical helmet and the belt are also inherited from Geometric fashion.

5. The iron kouros **M852**, possibly Apollo, from the temple of Epicurean Apollo at Bassae, dates from the beginning of the 7th century B.C.

6. The statuette of a young athlete (?) **B1700**, known as the "charioteer" marks a decisive departure from Geometric concepts. All the new elements which constitute 7th century art are concentrated in this figure, produced in an Elis workshop in the second quarter of the 7th century B.C.

Leg of a cast tripod, **B5314**; on the obverse which is, as usual, divided into sections, the scenes depicted from top to bottom are:

1. A horse and dog. 2. The chimaera, whose rendering suggests Assyrian prototypes. 3. A bull. 4. Remains of a serpent and curly locks (?) which might have been those of a gorgon. The other sides are decorated with spiral-meanders and leaf decoration. This exceptional work of the late 7th century B.C. was produced in Laconia.

Revetments of chests or larnakes, of furniture and maybe even of architectural elements bearing vegetal motifs, such as **M946**, **B4276**, **M209** and **B6183** on the bottom shelf, have been found in significant quantity at Olympia. Their dating and origin present many problems. Most probably they were produced in an eastern Ionian (Samian?) workshop, and the majority date from the second half of the 7th century B.C.

A fragment from the clothing of a statue, which was attached on a wooden core, **B1740**. First half of the 6th century B.C.

Above Case 7: Part of a clay sima, possibly from one of the Treasuries, first quarter of the 6th century B.C.

B1999. Bronze statuette of a warrior.

a) B1700. Bronze statuette of an athlete (?).

b) B4276. Bronze sheet with hammered decoration.

c) B5314. Part of a cast tripod leg with decoration.

a

b

c

M102. Bronze sheet with hammered decoration.

M112. Bronze sheet with hammered decoration.

B4422 + B5240. Bronze cauldron, with one of the five original protomes, the figure of a bull, still in position. (?) Late Hittite. End of the 8th century B.C. There is a Greek inscription on the lip: Sacred to Zeus.

B4999. Monumental hammered lion's head with engraved details, a late Hittite work of the 8th century B.C. It may have been the emblem for a shield, though some believe that it may have been part of the architectural decoration of a building and date it to the middle of the 7th century B.C.

Λ3. This lion, in limestone, served as the spout of a fountain; it is one of the earliest sculptures in stone to have been found at Olympia, and maybe one of the oldest in Greece. 680-670 B.C.

Case 8

Top shelf: **B1529**, a hammered sheet, depicting a warrior leaving for battle. This theme, much loved in Greek art, is frequently associated with specific heroes, Hector or Amphiaraos (see also **M78**, below, in the Wall Case). First quarter of the 6th century B.C.

B5555. Statuette of Silenos with prominent genitalia, represented as he was originally conceived of as a daemonic element of nature perpetually fruitful and fecund. Around mid-6th century B.C.

Hammered sheets **M108 + M205** depicting the blinding of Polyphemus. Odysseus, or one of his companions, holds the stake ready to plunge into the Cyclop's eye; it may be his foot which is depicted on the sheet **M205**. From an eastern-Ionian workshop, in the first decade of the 6th century B.C.

The female mask **B5099** may have been affixed to the head of a wooden statue of a goddess. The modelling is of unrivalled delicacy and sensitivity, and may be of Laconian origin, but with a suggestion of Ionian influence. 650-625 B.C.

Middle shelf: Other important works in the case include the dove, **M107**, which decorated the "omphalos" (central piece) of the yoke of a chariot (see the sheet **M102** on the same shelf); the sheet **M112** depicting a chariot race and **M359** with a lion devouring a deer, a familiar theme in Archaic art; lastly, the sheet **B5800** showing Herakles' struggle against the Hydra.

Above Case 8: The corner section of the clay sima from the Treasury of the Sicilians, dating from the second quarter of the 6th century B.C.

a

a) B5099. Hammered bronze
female mask.

b) M78. Bronze sheet with
hammered decoration.

b

Wall Cases

M78. Bronze sheet with a representation of a warrior, possibly Amphiaraos, bidding farewell to his familly before setting off to war. This is the work of an easten-Ionian workshop around 580 B.C. The usual paratactic arrangement of the figures in the early compositions is disturbed here by the backward turn of the hero, and by his waving gesture to the figures behind him. At the same time the purely narrative character of the composition is lost through the emerging dramatic content, conveyed in undertones in the calm bearing of the child, the suppressed smile and the meeting of glances.

M77. Bronze sheets with hammered representations in successive panels: a) two heroes and a female figure; b) Orestes killing Clytemnestra; behind him Electra applauds the deed while Aegisthus runs for protection at the altar; c) Theseus "abducts" Antiope, queen of the Amazons. From eastern Ionia, roughly contemporary with **M78**, this is a naive and lively piece of work.

B850. Hammered bronze sheet, showing a lion tearing a deer apart. To the right is an eagle with two of its young. This is a lively scene contrasting the idyllic with the cruel side of Nature. 675-650 B.C.

On the wall

Λ1. Colossal head of a goddess in limestone. This may have belonged to the cult statue of Hera in the Heraion. Pausanias tells us that Zeus, fully armed, stood next to the seated Hera. Some believe that the head belongs to a sphinx, and there are still other interpretations. The goddess wore a polos on her beautifully combed hair and possibly also a hairnet. The daemonic expression of the face is softened by a flush of maternal indulgence. It is a typical work of the Peloponnesian school from around 600 B.C.

Wall Case

B106. Hammered bronze sheet with a representation of a dragon attacking a winged ibex. Ionian workshop of the end of the 7th century B.C.

Wall Case

Three bronze sheets with hammered potrayals of animals, real or imaginary. From Ionian workshops.

B4348. Right and left of a plant motif, two sphinxes rampant. Rams and eagles. 625-600 B.C.

Λ1. Head of a goddess in limestone.

79

a

b

B4347. A griffin. 650-625 B.C.

B4174. Hind quarters of a boar, end of the 7th c. B.C.

Case 9

The reclining Silenus **B4232** holding a drinking horn in his hand is the work of a gifted craftsman, as are the similar figures **B4200** and **B4700.** They all decorated the rim of the same bronze vessel. They date from around 530-520 B.C.

The marching warrior **B5000** and the old man with his staff **B25** are amongst the most beautiful statuettes found in the sanctuary. Products of a Laconian craftsman around 550 B.C., they probably decorated the lip of an open vessel. Together with other figures, they may have made up a gathering of heroes, one of the many described in the epics.

The kore **B3004** was probably the handle of a small basin. She wears only a loincloth and shoes. This is a Peloponnesian work of the beginning of the 5th c. B.C.

Λ257. Stone kouros from Phygalia, possibly Apollo. His arms, the upper parts close to the torso, were bent forwards, and he certainly held some of the appropriate symbols. Around 570 B.C.

Λ256. Part of the torso of a kouros, from the harbour of Pheia, Elis, dated to the mid 6th century B.C.

Π2968. A section of the painted terracotta acroterion which decorated the pediment of an unidentified building, perhaps a Treasury of one of the cities of Magna Graecia, 550-525 B.C. (see the reconstruction).

On a pedestal on the north side of the hall

The crowning acroterion of the Heraion, in terracota (**Π2969**). It has been reassembled from many pieces (see also the coloured drawing). The rear side was so fashioned as to support the crowning ridge tile of the roof. It is a wonderful example of the exceptionally developed ceramic art of the later 7th century B.C. The intelligent alternation of the flat and the moulded surfaces of the disc and the harmonisation of the decorative elements with the shades of colour give the impression of perpetual motion. Because of this the acroterion, placed at the highest point of the temple, would have looked like the sun or a stellar emblem, burning and spinning. Unique in its size and "daemonic" in the archaic sense, the acroterion dates from the turn of the 7th century B.C.

Two painted clay antefixes from the Heraion.

a) Π2969. Terracotta acroterion from the Heraion.

b) Reconstruction of the terracotta acroterion from the Heraion.

B5000 Bronze statuette of a warrior.

81

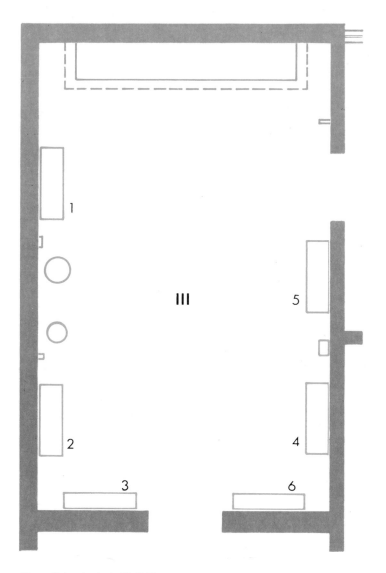

Plan of the Archaic Hall II.

ARCHAIC GALLERY II

Case 3

On the top and bottom shelves are various vessels from workshops in Elis, dating from the 7th and 6th centuries B.C.

On the middle shelf a large skyphos and lekythoi in the Attic black-figured style; most of the latter date from the first half of the 5th century B.C., i.e. the period when the style was in decline. The mythical themes they depict are of interest; Herakles, assisted by Athena, attempting to bind the Cretan Bull (**Π3230**); Herakles fighting the Amazons (**Π2970**); Dionysos with his thiasos (**Π1556**) etc.

Case 2

Decorative attachments from cauldrons and other vessels. Amongst them are many fragments of rod-bundle legs from tripod cauldron stands (see Archaic Gallery I, case 1). **B6115, B6100** and **B5570** on the middle shelf have a striking palmette final. A leg from an incense burner (**B1001**) with an unusual presentation, showing a child in the position of a jumper above a winged lion's foot; this is probably Etruscan, around 480-460 B.C. On the middle and bottom shelf lion's feet from tripods and other vessels (**Br.11554** and **B5758 + Br.1375**). Ram's head from a cauldron (**B5668**) of the early 6th century B.C. (top shelf).

Above the case 2: Terracotta palmette antefixe from the Gelan Treasury.

B7000. Tripod leg of cast bronze decorated on six successive panels:
1. A male figure holding a horse by the reins.
2. A scorpion above a lion.
3. Odysseus escaping from the cave of the Cyclop Poly-

B5570 Fragment from a bronze cauldron.

B6100. Fragment from a bronze cauldron.

a

b

a) Br.11554. Lion's foot from a bronze utensil.

b) B5758+Br.1375. Bronze basin.

phemus concealed under the belly of a ram. There is a bird above the ram.

4. A goat and a bird.
5. Two opposing, bickering birds.
6. The Gorgon and her offspring, Pegasos. A lizard is close to her head. The portrayal of chronologically separate episodes, from the same myth, is typical of Archaic art. Here – although this cannot be considered a variation of the myth – the Gorgon is shown already nursing Pegasos, even though tradition maintained that he was not born until after her beheading by Perseus. Corinthian workshop, around 600 B.C.

Br.13436. Cauldron with the inscription: *Sacred to Zeus.*

Π140. Clay perrirhanterion from Skillous (Babes). Its stand bears impressed decoration of horsemen and rosettes in successive registers. End of the 7th century B.C.

On the wall

Part of the painted terracotta pediment of the Gelan Treasury. Because of the perfect technique, the colours are excellently preserved. Around 560 B.C.
Wall Case: B108. A horse's head on a hammered bronze sheet, probably a shield device. Around 500 B.C.

Case 1

On the two uppermost shelves fragments of terracotta figurines and protomes are displayed. Many were found on the site of the New Museum, for example the head of the young man (**Π434**), radiant with spiritual maturity, dating from the first decades of the 5th century B.C.; the "daedalic" goddesses (**Π170a-b, Π370a**), shown in the rigid monumental modelling of the 7th century B.C.. The terracotta female head (**T1**) possibly that of a sphinx-acroterion from the Gelan Treasury, has a lively expression of complacent charm; it is a work from Magna Graecia from the decade 530-520 B.C. Lastly, there are poros-stone fragments of relief birds (**Λ33, Λ34** and **Λ35**), which were part of the sculptured pedimental decoration of the Treasury of Byzantion.

On the bottom shelf are fragments from the base of a cauldron (**B6124 + Br.13530**) and of architectural revetments.

Above Case 1: TC111772 + T7. Terracotta sphinx, probably an acroterion from a Treasury. It is Corinthian work of the mid-6th century B.C.

T1. Terracotta female head.

85

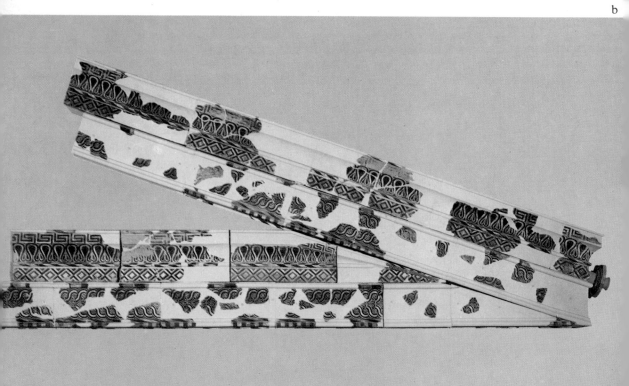

Restoration of the entablature with the pediment of the Treasury of the Megarians. On the pediment, which was of soft local limestone, 5.70 m. long and 0.75 m. high, is depicted the struggle of the gods and the giants, a popular theme in Greek art. According to Pausanias, a shield crowned the pediment, bearing an inscription that the Megarians had dedicated the Treasury from the spoils taken from the Corinthians. The inscription: Of the *Megarians* on the epistyle was cut in Roman times.

There were originally eleven figures on the pediment; the giants, Zeus, Athena, Herakles, as well as Poseidon and Ares, supported in battle respectively by sea monsters and serpents. The only one still relatively complete is the giant at the centre of the struggle. When they were discovered, many of the fragments preserved traces of their original paintwork. The work dates from the late Archaic period, around 520 B.C.

B2360. A battering ram in bronze. It is the only example of this siege weapon to have survived from antiquity. On both sides there is a stylised representation of the animal from which it takes its name. The wooden trunk is missing. Its worn, bent teeth show that it had been used before being dedicated in the Sanctuary. It dates from the first half of the 5th century B.C.

a) Restoration of part of the entablature with the pediment from the Megarian treasury.

b) Angular part of the painted terracotta pediment of the Gelan treasury.

Case 5

Top shelf: The statuette of Zeus **B3010**, who was most probably clutching thunder bolts in each hand, dates from about 520 B.C., as does the figure of the goddess with the flower **B5325**. An example of Peloponnesian workmanship, it must have formed the base of a vessel. The sphinx **B5300** also decorated a vessel of some kind; it is a lovely work of the last quarter of the 6th century B.C. from a Laconian atelier. The woman's head **B152**, hammered on an cut-out sheet is also a late Archaic piece. The slanting eye, stubby nose and fleshy cheeks are typical of Ionian ateliers; this example, however, is imbued with the spirit of Western Ionia, that is, Magna Graecia.

Middle shelf: Bronze jewellery from the Geometric to Roman periods. Buckles from the mid-6th century B.C. (**B4229**) and 5th century B.C. (**B1420 + B1608**). A series of pins showing the stages in their evolution. **Br.1016.** Geometric hair rings **Br.4277**, hair rings from the Classical era. **Br.6251**, 7th century B.C. buckle. Buckle **Br.3605** is a Phrygian and **Dι.439** is a work of the 2nd century B.C. **BΕ.868**, bronze bracelet from the 6th century B.C. **V9**, silver bracelet

B2360. Bronze battering-ram.

87

a) B152. Female head, hammered
on bronze sheet.

b) B5300. Bronze sphinx.

c) B5325. Bronze statuette of
a goddess.

from the end of the 6th or beginning of the 5th century B.C.;
its gilded finials are in the form of snakes' heads. Phrygian
buckle, **B8545**, from the 7th century B.C. **B5662**, bronze
buckle decorated with a cock from a Laconian workshop of
the first half of the 6th century B.C. **Br.1356**, bronze bracelet
of the "illyrian type" of the early 7th century B.C. **B4372**,
B4620, **B4626** and **B4373**, bronze rings of the Roman era.
The bezels bear the impressions of a sphinx, Hermes, a Muse
playing a kithara, Aphrodite holding a mirror. Bottom shelf:
Various bronze vessels. Middle shelf: Strainer **B5504** with a
delicate vegetal decoration and haldle with goose-head finial.

Λ4, Λ5. Small statue of a peplos-clad figure and part of
a lion in Laconian marble. The robed lady, together with
two other similar figures, stood upright on the lion's
back, supporting the basin of a perrirhanterion. These
and the limestone lion Λ3 (Archaic Gallery I) are the only
examples of large-scale sculpture in stone from the second half of the 7th century B.C.

On the wall:

Clay simae and antefixes from the Archaic buildings of
the Altis.

Case 4

Corinthian aryballoi and other vases from workshops in
Elis or Laconia. Clay house models (middle shelf). Laconian kylix **K1292**, dating from around 530 B.C. On the
inside Zeus and Hera are portrayed seated on a throne.
Behind them is an eagle, the symbol of the god, and in
front of them rests of a male figure, possibly Hermes or
Ganymede. On the outside of the vase traces of an incised
votive inscription.

Case 6

Bronze handles and griffins' or lion's paws from vessels.
Parts of the rims of cauldrons with feet of walking figures.

a

b

c

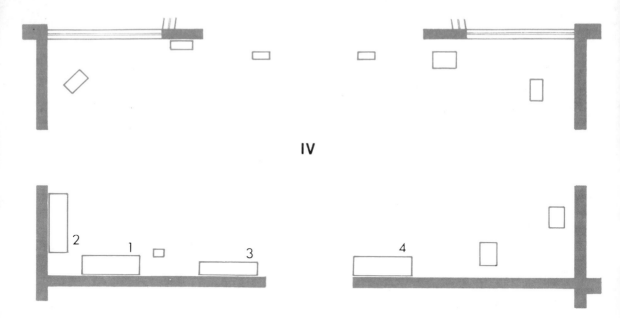

IV

Plan of the Early Classical-Classical Hall.

EARLY CLASSICAL
AND CLASSICAL GALLERY

If we exclude the large scuplted compositions of the temple of Zeus and the much later Nike of Paionios, works of the 5th century B.C. – the Classical period of Greek art – are remarkably few, especially since the sanctuary was flourishing at that time. According to ancient writers, the site was inundated with statues of gods, heroes and victors in the Games. Most of these were cast in bronze by the great artists of the day, amongst them Pheidias, Myron, Kalamis, Onatas, Pythagoras and Polykleitos. Not one has survived today, all that remains are a few fragments and several inscribed bases, attesting that a statue by a famous sculptor once stood there. Not even a single Roman copy of any of these works has survived.

Small works in bronze are equally rare. Since they were on public view, they later became easy targets for plunder, either for their artistic merit or for the value of the metal.

T2. A terracotta group depicting Zeus and Ganymede, probably the acroterion of a temple. The god, a traveller's knotted staff in his hand, leads the son of the king of Troy to Olympus where the gods would make him their cup-bearer and bestow on him the gift of eternal youth. Ganymede holds a cock, symbol of the love which his beauty awoke in the god's heart. The resolute satisfied expression on the face of the older man contrasts with the dreamy and carefree eyes of the youth. This is the first time that the psychology of age is presented in Greek art. It is a magnificent work from a Corinthian atelier, 480-470 B.C.

TC1798a-b + TC1800. Crouching terracotta lion of the mid-5th century B.C.

Free-standing Case

Two helmets. **M9** is Corinthian and **M844** Etruscan. They bear the same inscription engraved on their left sides: *To Zeus from Hieron, son of Deinomenes, and the Syracusans after their victory over the Tyrrhenians at Cumae.* The battle of Cumae took place in 474 B.C.; these helmets, no doubt part of the booty, were offered as votives in the Sanctuary of Zeus by Hieron, tyrant of Syracuse, and his fellow citizens. There is another Etruscan helmet, with the same inscription, in the British Museum.

Free-standing Case

B2600. The inscription on the left side of this plain but priceless helmet: *Miltiades dedicated this to Zeus,* attests that it is a votive of the renowned Athenian general. Both the type of helmet and the style of lettering confirm that it was in fact the very one worn by Miltiades at the battle of Marathon and which he presented to Zeus as a thank-offering after his victory over the Persians.

B5100. Bronze helmet of eastern origin, perhaps Assyrian. It has the same historical interest as **B2600** since, according to the inscription, it was an offering of the Athenians from the booty captured in the Persian Wars: *The Athenians took* [this helmet] *from the Medes* [and dedicated it] *to Zeus.* It is the only authenticated booty to have survived from that dramatic struggle.

A100. This larger than life-size statue of Zeus in Pentelic marble, may be an offering from the Roman general Mummius. It is a copy made in the 2nd century A.D. of a mid-5th century B.C. original.

T3. Terracotta statue of a warrior. It formed one of a group of two or more figures engaged in combat, of which only fragments have survived. It is not known whether it belonged to a pediment, or whether it was one of a multitude of many-figured offerings to the shrine. It is of exceptionally high standard, from a Peloponnesian atelier around 480 B.C.

A109. Statue of Zeus in Pentelic marble, a free copy of an original, probably in bronze, which would have dated to around 450 B.C. The competent but unimaginative working of the marble shows that it was made under the first Antonine emperors. Recently it has been suggested that the statue belonged to the sculpted decoration of the Nymphaion, founded by Herodus Atticus.

A108. Statue of Zeus in Pentelic marble, of the Dresden type. It is an exceptionally good copy, made in the second

T2. Terracotta group of Zeus with Ganymede.

B5100. Bronze Assyrian (?) helmet, taken as booty in the Persian wars.

B2600. Miltiades' helmet.

*a) T3. Terracotta statue of
a warrior.*

*b) Λ108. Marble statue of Zeus of
the «Dresden» type.*

c) Λ109. Marble statue of Zeus.

a

b

c

95

century A.D. of an original, probably in bronze, dating from around 430 B.C. Some consider that the statue represents Zeus Chthonios or Pluto. According to a recent theory, this statue, like **Λ109** above, was part of the sculpted decoration of the Nymphaion.

Case 4

Iron keys of various types for fastening door latches; farming and quarrying tools; axes, ploughshares, pick-axes, pair of scales (**E197a**) and bridles (**E155, E195**); iron skewers, one of which is inscribed: Of the *Olympian Zeus*, showing that it was either an offering or part of the equipment of the priesthood.

Case 1

Top shelf: The eagle **B4916** topped a sceptre which must have belonged to a relatively large statue of Zeus, dated to the decade 470-460 B.C. The statuette of Zeus **B800** holding a thunderbolt in his right hand and perhaps an eagle in his left is of the same date. This statuette along with a series of other found at Olympia, the oldest of which dates to the last decades of the 6th century B.C., are of a type inherited from the earliest Archaic period which remained popular until the latter years of the 5th century B.C. Two other statues of Zeus, **B5500 + B5778** and **B5550** fall into this category. The first, with an indecipherable dedicatory inscription, is somewhat earlier than the second.

The statuette **B6300** of a naked, bearded man, standing on a stepped base, may represent Zeus. The god held a sceptre, or perhaps a spear, in his left hand and may have had a bowl in his right. It dates from 480-470 B.C. The statuette **B4310** perhaps depicts Hermes or a hunter or shepherd. This is an exceptional piece from a Peloponnesian workshop, dated to around 480 B.C. The cap and chlamys, clumsily executed, were added later, for unknown reasons.

The statuette of Athena, **M767**, from Prasidaki, is also from the first quarter of the 5th century B.C.

The statuette **B1601** depicts Pan. According to tradition, worship of the goat-faced god originated in Arcadia and in time spread over the whole of Greece. He was worshipped at Olympia even in later times, and two altars were dedicated to him. The god, shown dancing, holds the staff in his left hand and appears to be snapping the fingers of his right. His facial features have been softened, and his expression glows with the spirituality of the clas-

B5500+B5778. Bronze statuette of Zeus.

sical period. It dates from around 430 B.C.

Second shelf: Only an ear and one horn, **M888**, have survived from the bronze bull dedicated by the Eretrians after their victory over the Athenians at the beginning of the 5th century B.C. Its base, bearing the legend: *Philesios made this; the Eretrians dedicated it to Zeus,* can still be seen in its original position, northeast of the temple of Zeus.

The corner antefix **Π3321** came from the roof of Pheidias' workshop.

Above Case 1

TC1093-4598. Terracotta dolphin leaping out of the waves, possibly an acroterion. It dates from around 400 B.C.

Case 2

T6. The head of a terracotta statue of Athena. The many fragments with which it was found suggest that Athena was one of a multi-figured composition offered to the Sanctuary. On her beautifully arranged locks she wore an Attic helmet with a crest, no longer preserved. The influence of the Peloponnesian school of around 490 B.C. is very evident; the head, with its lively vigorous expression and the all-pervasive spirituality, is one of the most typical creations of the Severe style.

Fragments from a terracotta group of a Satyr and Maenad. Upper and middle shelves **TC3529, TC1048 (K172)**. Dating from around 500 B.C. It may have been the acroterion of a Treasury (see the drawing to the right).

Locks of hair and various limbs from bronze statues, large numbers of which filled the sacred Alsos.

B5110. Two lions lacerating a deer — the handle of a sumptuous basin, around 480 B.C.

Free-standing Case

B1000. Small bronze horse once harnessed to a quadriga (a four-horse chariot). It is probably the work of an Argive sculptor who here portrays the noble animal with love and skill. About 470 B.C.

Case 3

The clay moulds for drapery folds, both large and small, are amongst the most interesting finds from the sanctuary. They also constitute conclusive evidence that the

a) B1000. Bronze statuette of a horse.

b) B5110. Bronze utensil handle: two lions tearing a deer apart.

a

b

99

Finds from the workshop of Pheidias.

a,b) Tools.

c) Terracotta ornament mould.

d) Π3653. Pheidias' wine cup.

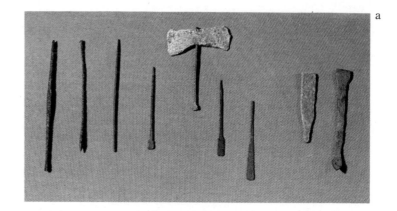

a

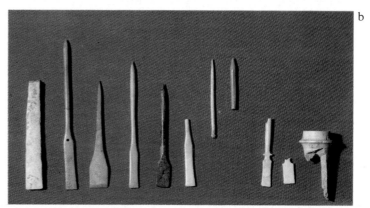

b

c

d

spots where they were found was that occupied by the workshop in which Pheidias made the chryselephantine statue of Zeus. The larger moulds shaped the himation which clothed it, others were used for the smaller figures, such as the Nike held by the god, or the Hours and Graces which, according to Pausanias, decorated the back of his throne. Other moulds of different shapes were used for the decorative parts in glass – palmettes, leaves etc. There is still glass in one of them. Similar significance is attached to the other remnants of materials employed –metals and ivory– and to the large numbers of bone tools and a bronze goldsmith's hammer. By far the most moving find from the workshop was the small black-painted wine cup inscribed with the words: *I belong to Pheidias,* on the underside of the base. These letters are almost certainly in the hand of this great artist who set his indelible seal on the art of the 5th century B.C.

Terracotta mould of drapery, from Pheidias' workshop.

Sherds from a kalyx-krater, painted by Kleophon around 435-430 B.C., depict Nike and a kithara player, though only parts of his instrument remain. These too were found in Pheidias' workshop. It is worth mentioning that the ceramic finds from the workshop date from between 440 and 430 B.C. while the infill, which covered it after it had been abandoned, dates from between 430 and 410 B.C. Therefore, the chryselephantine statue of Zeus must have been finished by 410 B.C. at the latest. This evidence conclusively solves a problem which scholars have debated for years; whether Pheidias worked at Olympia before or after he made the chryselephantine statue of Athena Parthenos, which was finished in 438 B.C.

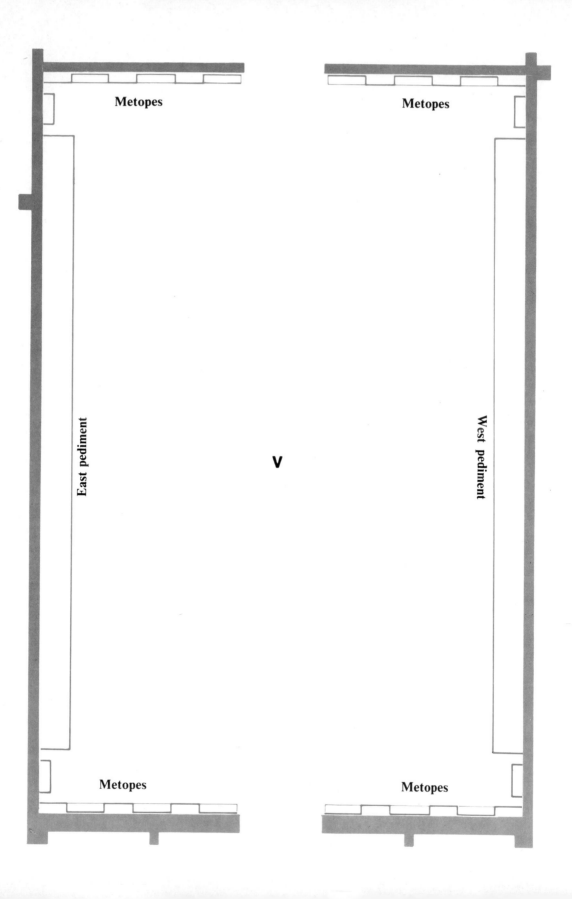

Metopes

Metopes

East pediment

West pediment

V

Metopes

Metopes

GALLERY OF SCULPTURES
FROM THE TEMPLE OF ZEUS

Cosmogonic changes took place at the turn of the 6th century B.C., reaching their highest expression in the period after the Persian wars, the richest, most heroic and happiest era of Greek history. The period is something of a watershed, for it saw the perfection of the most profound changes in the life of the Greeks: in religion, the re-evaluation of the way in which the gods and heroes were perceived; in politics, the reforms which permitted the establishment of democracy; in philosophy, the shift of interest from the outside world, which until then had been dominant, to the study of man and the fathomless depths of his soul; in literature, the birth and flowering of tragedy and prose, and finally, in art. It is at this time that the carefree Archaic smile was finally erased from the faces of statues, to be replaced by a serious and meditative expression suggesting the moral principles of moderation by which this generation, ripening into maturity, would try to live. All these changes are mirrored in the art of the time, especially in the sculptures of the temple of Zeus at Olympia which represent the most mature and most exciting period of Greek art.

But there is another reason also to pay particular attention to the sculptures on the temple of Zeus amongst the works of this period. Very few examples of monumental sculpture survive from this extraodinary era: The Poseidon of Artemision and the Charioteer of Delphi are perhaps the best known. And then, all at once, the rich and intricate group from Olympia, consisting of forty-two figures from the pediment, twelve metopes and the lion-head spouts, fills the gap; it is the most eloquent expression of the Severe style, as the art of the first half of the 5th century B.C. more precisely of the period from 480-450 B.C., is rightly called.

Plan of the Hall of Sculptures from the temple of Zeus.

The east pediment from the temple of Zeus. The chariotrace between
Pelops and Oinomaus.

The west pediment from the temple of Zeus. The Centauromachy.

The central part of the east pediment. Zeus stands in the middle with Oinomaus and Sterope on his right and Pelops and Hippodameia on his left. At the two ends, the quadrigas of the contestants with their servants.

The construction of the temple of Zeus began about 470 B.C. and must have been completed at the latest by 456 B.C. when, according to the surviving inscription, the Spartans erected a golden shield on the gable of the eastern pediment as a thank-offering for their victory over the Argives, Athenians and Ionians at the battle of Tanagra. Indeed, this shield is mentioned by Pausanias (5.10.4).

The east pediment of the temple depicted the chariot race between Pelops and Oinomaos, the west the struggle between the Lapiths and Centaurs. The gigantic figures of Parian marble filled the huge triangular space of each pediment (26.39 m. long and 3.47 m. high). Above the entrance of the pronaos and opisthodomos the metopes were decorated with the Labours of Herakles, in six panels alternating with triglyphs.

After thirty years study of material in the Museum storerooms of Olympia, in the sanctuary and also in the basements of the Louvre, about three hundred more fragments have been added to the sculptures. Now, noticeably more complete, they provide a much more accurate picture of their original stance and position.

This new reconstruction of the pediments and metopes lacks the shining weapons borne by the heroes and the chariots with their accoutrements which completed the composition and indeed brought it to life. It is also devoid of all but the merest traces of the bright red and blue paint used to colour the eyes and hair of the statues in particular.

EAST PEDIMENT

On the east pediment, Zeus, the guardian and sovereign of the temple, occupied the centre of the composition; his original height was about 3,15 m. (he now stands at 2.91 m.). In his left hand he held a thunderbolt, which has not been preserved. On either side stood the two heroes of the myth, Oinomaos king of Pisa (about 2.85 m. high) and Pelops (height 2.77 m.). The latter, the legitimate son of Tantalus, came from distant Lydia to challenge Oinomaos for possession of his daughter, Hippodameia. It was a fight to the death since Oinomaos, informed by an oracle that he would be killed by his daughter's husband, would only give her in marriage to the man who, granted a head start, succeeded in outriding his own unbeaten horses, a gift from his natural father Ares. Thirteen brave youths had already lost their lives before Pelops took up the challenge with the divine horses bestowed on him by his natural father Poseidon. Oinomaos was defeated; Pe

The upper portion of the statue of Zeus.

The head of Oinomaus.

109

The head of the soothsayer from the left half of the east pediment.

lops married Hippodameia and their offspring were the first of the Pelopid dynasty from which the entire peninsula, until then called Apia, took the name Peloponnese, the isle of Pelops.

The young Hippodameia stands at Pelops side, clothed as for a wedding in an austere doric peplos. Her left arm, lifting the peplos, is a gesture associated with marriage, and when it occurs in wedding scenes it is known as the "unveiling".

To balance this, Sterope, wife of Oinomaos, stands by his side, her peplos loosely draped and hands crossed on her breast, the left perhaps straying towards her chin, betraying the anxiety welling up inside her. Next to the heroines are the chariots of the two rivals with their servants and, seated on the ground, the soothsayers, possibly Iamos and Amythaon (some say Klytios), the mythical forebears of the two priestly families, which traditionally supplied Olympia with its priesthood – a hereditary office. Finally, the semi-reclining figures in the corners of the pediment are, according to Pausanias (5.10.6 ff.), the two rivers which watered the plain where the sanctuary stood, the Alpheios and the Kladeos. Following the practice of the time, they were shown in human form, since man and nature were still regarded as an integral whole.

The arrangement of the figures on the pediment, a subject of protracted discussion amongst scholars, is here based mainly on the location in which each of the large fragments was discovered. For, it is more than likely that in the earthquake which destroyed the temple in the 6th century A.D. the massive, heavy figures would have fallen more or less directly to the ground below their original position on the pediment. Furthermore, some of the statues whose height, torsion or other traits are alone decisive for determining their original position were indeed found on the ground beneath the place they first stood – Zeus, the river gods and the chariots for certain.

Controversy centres still only on the positioning of the heroic couples to the right and left of Zeus, and on the proper identification of the two women, so that Hippodameia may correctly take her place beside her betrothed and Sterope by her husband. Doubt was provoked by an obscurity noticed by scholars in the remarks of Pausanias (5.10.6) who says that Oinomaos was *"on the right of Zeus"*; they point out that he has not made clear whether "right" is in relation to the spectator or to the god. But Pausanias certainly meant the latter, since he goes on to tell us that Oinomaos' rival, Pelops, was to the left side of Zeus.

Another, totally different interpretation of Pausanias'

remarks cannot be upheld, namely that the god's head was inclined to the right, that is towards the hero he favoured, in this case Pelops. This would mean that the loser in the contest, Oinomaos, could not possibly have occupied a position on the right. But the tiny portion of the god's neck to have survived gives no certain indication as to how he held his head.

As this reconstruction places them, the spears of the two heroes (on either side of the god) accentuate Zeus' dominant position in the composition and stress his unseen presence. If, on the other hand, their positions were to be reversed, not only would the spears extend beyond the border of the pediment, but they would also isolate the heroes from the figures with which they were associated.

The placing of the couple Pelops and Hippodameia to the left of Zeus also justifies the presence of the attendant below the right-hand chariot next to Hippodameia. According to the conditions of the race Pelops was to have as charioteer none other than Hippodameia, whose beauty was to have distracted him during the contest. Oinomaos, on the other hand, retained the accustomed services of Myrtilos, who may perhaps be the kneeling figure in front of the left-hand chariot, while the other man behind him may have been one of Oinomaos' servants, or vice versa.

One further difference of opinion concerns the naming of the two rivers in the corners of the pediment. In his description Pausanias named Kladeos as the occupant of the corner to the right of Zeus while Alpheios was to the left. The second figure, more compactly built and robust, seems better to fit the image of the tireless river lover who, as myth recounts, chased the nymph Arethusa and lay with her in the spring which bears her name at Syracuse. Lastly, the youth to the right, seated between the soothsayer and the river god, brings to mind the hero Arkas as he is represented on Arcadian coins. If this identification is valid then the young man's position next to Alpheios is justified, since the river's sources lie in Arcadia, his homeland.

a) *The attendant in front of Oinomaus' quadriga.* $\longrightarrow$

b) *The servant-girl in front of Pelops' quadriga.* $\longrightarrow$

111

b

c

a) The servant behind Oinomaus' quadriga.

b) The youth (Arkas ?) behind the soothsayer from the right half of the east pediment.

c) The head of the soothsayer from the right half of the east pediment.

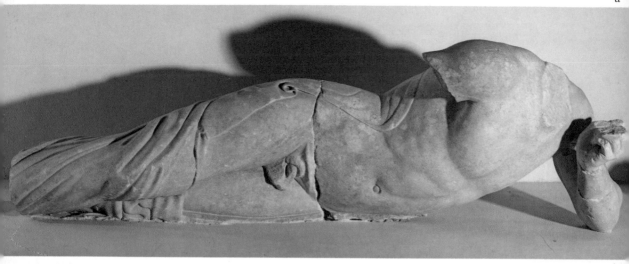

a

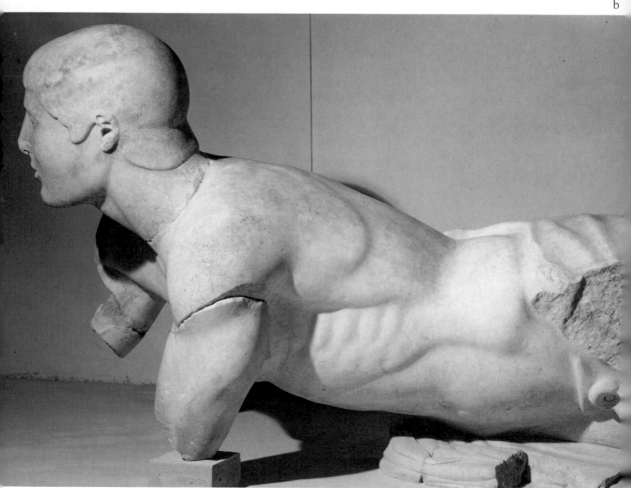

b

116

WEST PEDIMENT

The west pediment shows the drunken Centaurs, invited to the wedding of Peirithous, king of the Lapiths, violating the sacred law of hospitality by attempting to abduct the beautiful Lapith women. In the ensuing clash the combatants are shown in groups of twos and threes. At the centre of the composition Apollo (about 3.15 m. high), god of reason and order in the world, intervenes to punish the offenders, his bow in his left hand (only the sockets which held it survive). To the right of the god Peirithous falls on Eurytion, king of the Centaurs, who had grabbed the young nymph Deidameia with hands and feet, to the left Theseus (pres. height 2.51 m.), friend of Peirithous, is about to inflict a mortal wound on another Centaur to free a Lapith from his violent embrace.

Similarly dramatic clashes occupy the whole pediment, while in each corner, reclining on the ground two Lapiths, follow the struggle anxiously. Of these four figures, only the first from the right is contemporary with the other sculptures of the pediment, though her right arm, originally of Parian marble has been replaced in Pentelic, possibly after earthquake damage. The three other figures are also in Pentelic marble; the first on the left must have been made in the 4th century B.C. while the other two show stylistic traits of the 1st century B.C. They replaced originals damaged by one of the earthquakes recorded in literary sources and reflected in the evidence of excavations.

The outcome of the battle between Lapiths and Centaurs has been settled since Apollo's right hand rests protectively in Peirithous' shoulder. *"Epidexios Apollo"*, the god who extends his right hand – as the ancients dubbed him – was viewed as a benevolent deity who always intervened on the side of the innocent.

The difference in the conception underlying the two pediments is worthy of comment. On the east the figures, whether standing, kneeling or recumbent, are not connected with each other; motionless, each is shut within himself, an entity in his own right. Their contours are dominated by the straight line; vertical in the figures in the centre and horizontal in those at the sides. In their tragic immobility and isolation the figures all seem instinctively to anticipate the dramatic ending in an atmosphere charged with a breathless hush, the calm before the storm.

This expression of the tragic, which we meet here in monumental sculpture for the first time and which lurks behind the ill-omened immobility of the heroic figures, is

a) The river god (Kladeos ?) in the left corner of the east pediment.

b) The river god (Alpheios ?) in the right corner of the east pediment.

117

*The central part of the west pediment. Apollo stands in the middle
with Peirithous and the group of Eurytion and Deidamia on his right
and Theseus and the group of the Centaur and the Lapith woman
on his left. Other groups of figures to the sides.*

The upper part of the statue of Apollo.

most intense in the seated figure of the aged soothsayer behind the chariot on the right. In his face, where years of experience have left their wrinkles and, even more, in his eyes deep in thought, one reads the drama which rent the house of Oinomaos and its tragic outcome.

By contrast, on the west pediment the battle is raging and nears its climax. The outlines of the opponents locked in turbulent struggle cross and re-cross in an unending pattern of oblique and wavy lines which start from one corner of the pediment, reach a peak in the centre and fade out in the opposite corner, from which they sweep back in a ceaseless tide. The huge powerful contenders echo the epic struggle of man, represented by the Lapiths, against the unreasoning, chaotic and untameable forces of nature, represented in the ancient myth by the Centaurs.

The titanic vision of the separate worlds of Man and Centaur here acquires a new dimension. The idealistic faces of the Lapiths, both men and women, contrast strongly with the repulsive mis-shapen ones of the Centaurs with their bestial expressions, lascivious eyes, low brows foreheads and thick sensual lips, all conveying unbridled lust. It is one further depiction of the deep changes occurring at this time in the life of the Greeks; the myth has been elevated, from a simple narrative, into a symbol of the new Hellenic ideal, the moral standard of virtue and moderation. This ideal, systematically nurtured by Games sponsored at the sanctuaries, and especially those of Olympia, was not limited to the training of the body, but was diffused through all human effort, moral, intellectual and artistic.

Here, Zeus and Apollo as the original adjudicators of the Games and the first hellanodikai, watch over the games, not aimed simply at awarding prizes to the winners but also at the cultivation of a competitive spirit in every sphere of higher ambition and creativity. No more fitting nor more remarkable setting than the majestic temple of Zeus could have been chosen by the priests of Olympia from which to proclaim the deeper meaning of the games which, for generations, moved the people of the ancient world.

a

a) *Eurytion and Deidamia.*

b) *Theseus, the Centaur and the Lapith woman.*

b

a) Lapith and Centaur from the right half of the west pediment. →

b) Lapith and Centaur from the right half of the west pediment. →

c) Lapith from the left half of the west pediment. →

a

b

c
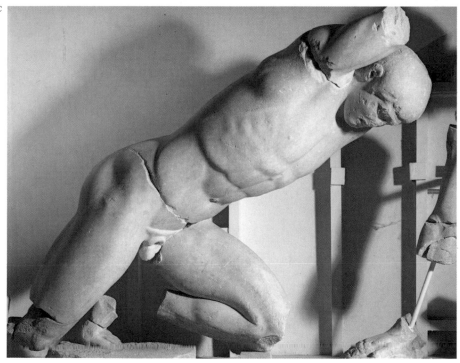

a) *Lapith woman from the group in the left half of the west pediment.*

b) *The two Lapith women in the left corner of the west pediment.*

c) *The two Lapith women in the right corner of the west pediment.*

b

c
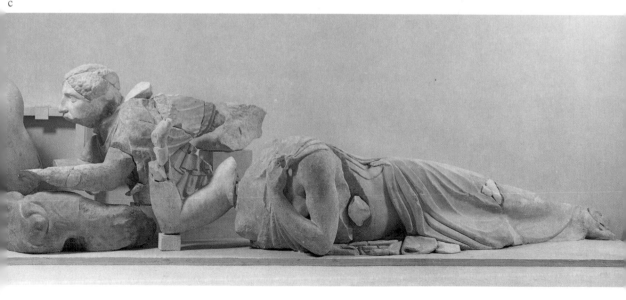

The head of the first Lapith woman.

The head of the second Lapith woman.

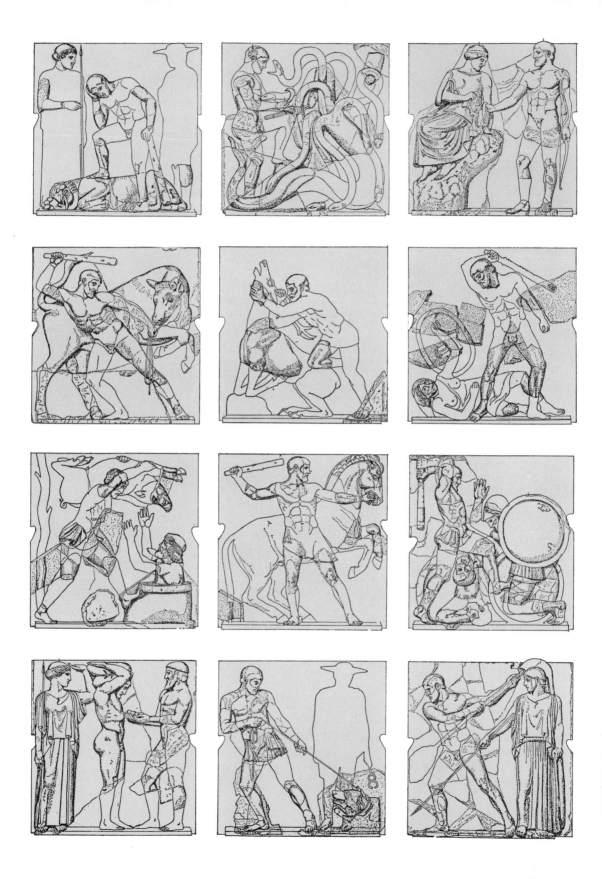

THE METOPES

Herakles is of as much importance at Olympia as Pelops. While the latter is shown as the founder of the Pelopid dynasty and represents the Mycenaean phase of the sanctuary, in mythology Herakles is the founder of the athletic contests in the Altis and is associated with the ancient cults which represent its Dorian phase. It was therefore natural that the Labours of Herakles, which stirred every Greek, should form one of the temple's decorative themes. They, together with the chariot race of Pelops and Oinomaos and the Centauromachy, made up an expressive trilogy, an inspiration to those competitors at the sacred site of Olympia.

The display of the metopes on the narrow walls of this Gallery in the museum corresponds to the order described by Pausanias. On the west side is the Nemean Lion, the Lernaean Hydra, the Stymphalian Birds, the Cretan Bull, the Kerynean Hind and the Girdle of the Amazon; on the east the Erymanthian Boar, the Mares of Diomedes, the Cattle of Geryon, Atlas, Cerberus and the Cleansing of the Augean Stables. The designs of some of the scenes follow the ancient iconographic tradition, on the contrary, others, bursting with a freshly-found strength, blaze new trails bearing the message of the generation born after the Persian wars.

In the first scene Herakles, a young man, is not shown struggling with the lion, as in the older tradition, but with the beast already dead. Exhausted, the first wrinkle creasing his brow, his head rests contemplatively on his crooked right arm. Next to him, tender-eyed Athena and behind him Hermes (who has not been preserved), stand by him in the difficult tasks he has yet to perform. Such a depiction of the tired hero is unexpected, especially in this period overflowing with energy and with an unquenchable thirst for action. Its creator was far ahead of his time; for the underlying concept, full of tragic pathos, was a precursor of much that was to come. The theme of the tired hero does not reappear for a hundred years; it resurfaces in the early Hellenistic period when the Greek world was indeed exhausted by the tribulations which beset it at that time.

Whereas the composition of the next metope, the slaying of the Lernaean Hydra, does not depart from the older models, a new spirit permeates the depiction of the Stymphalian Birds. Here, Athena, barefoot and without her weapons, is seated with youthful grace on a rock, as though expecting flowers from her lover and not the dead birds which were the fruit of Herakles' labours. This idyl-

The head of Herakles from the metope with Cerberus.

131

a) The metope with the Lion of Nemea.

b) The head of Athena from the metope of the Lion of Nemea.

c) The head of Herakles from the metope of the Lion of Nemea.

b

c

The head of Herakles from the Augean Stables metope.

lic presentation supplants the older heroic content of the myth; a lyric quality has replaced the epic. Here, as in the metope depicting the slaying of the Nemean Lion, the dominance of the vertical and horizontal lines and the total absence of motion, remind one of the composition of the east pediment. The same refreshing strength triumphs in the next of the Labours, the struggle of Herakles with the Cretan bull; the oblique counter-balance of the powerful beast with the hero recalls the highly dramatic figures locked in combat on the west pediment. In contrast the Kerynean Hind and the Battle with the Amazons, the two last metopes on the eastern side, remain faithful to older iconographical models.

The same general characteristics can be seen in the metopes on the western side. Some are faithful copies of older models (the Erymanthian Boar, Geryon). Others are tinged with the awakening of the spirit of things yet to come, some akin to the characteristics of the east pediment, others displaying an affinity with the west pediment. Although very fragmentary, the harmonius balance between vertical and horizontal lines of horse and hero are clear in the metope depicting Herakles and the Mares of Diomedes, just as they are in the figures of the east pediment. The same is true of the rigid upstanding figures in the metope of Atlas. Here Herakles, though the greatest of heroes, is barely able to support the weight of the sky, while the goddess has only to raise her left hand to relieve his burden. The difference between divinity and mortal is expressed simply, without rhetorical flourishes. But another aspect of the presentation of the myth is worth observing. While in older versions Atlas sought some ruse to leave Herakles sypporting the weight of the sky forever, now he willingly offers him the apples. The attempt to rid the tale of any trace of trickery is obvious, a purge characteristic of the age.

Finally, in the two metopes depicting the bringing of Cerberus from the underworld and the cleansing of the Augean stables, Herakles springs boldly to the left in strong contrast to the immobility and upright stance of Hermes in the first metope (though only the merest trace of his figure survives) and of Athena in the second. The spirit of the composition of the west pediment is all-pervasive.

The metope of the Cleansing of the Augean Stables.

The metope of the Cretan Bull.

The metope of the Stymphalian birds.

The metope of Atlas.

Herakles from the Atlas metope.

THE LION-HEAD WATERSPOUTS

The sculpted decoration of the temple was completed by the lion-head waterspouts carved in Parian marble, while the rest of the building was of the local shell limestone. In their monumental character, quality of workmanship and expressive force they equal the other temple sculpture. Since they were positioned at the highest point of the long sides, they bore the brunt of the earthquake shocks sustained by the temple throughout antiquity. Each time one fell, it was replaced in Pentelic not Parian marble, and each time in the prevailing style of the period, as was the case with the corner figures of the west pediment.

Nine stylistic groupings suggest that waterspouts were replaced on at least nine separate occasions, over the centuries, from the erection of the temple in 456 B.C. until the cessation of the Games in A.D. 393 and later, until the 6th century A.D., when the temple was destroyed by an earthquake which affected the whole of the northwest Peloponnese. Several of the many waterspouts have survived almost intact, but only four are on display, one at either end of each pediment. Amongst the other artistic treasures of the Museum the lion-head spouts themselves offer a full and vivid picture of the development of Greek sculpture from the period of the Severe style, to which the first belong, to the Late Roman period.

THE ARTIST

Pausanias' statement (5.10.8 ff.) that Paionios of Mende in Chalkidike created the east pediment and Alkamenes of Athens the west has always seemed of dubious veracity. Today scholars are unanimous in agreeing that the information given to the traveller by his guides at Olympia was erroneous. The style of Paionios (known from the marble Nike in the Museum) and of Alkamenes, pupil of Pheidias, both of whom employ fluid lines and softly yielding masses, is a totally different mode of artistic expression from the severe, stalwart, almost square figures of the pediments.

At this point, however, the unanimity of scholars breaks down. Simply because these works bear all the characteristics of the great schools of the age, they are attributed in turn to one and then to another craftsman, and the dissension continues. The debate is likely to remain unresolved, since these sculptures, though bearing the stamp of the cosmogonic changes experienced by the generation after the Persian wars, do not allow us to trace

Lion-head waterspouts from the temple of Zeus.

either forerunners or successors in any school. They remain isolated amongst the artistic currents of the 5th century B.C.

The artist who designed the figures, and there is no doubt that only one person is involved, was quite obviously influenced by the spirit of Attic tragedy and of large-scale painting which flowered in his time. With wonderful eloquence he managed to convey not just the dramatic isolation and tension in immobility before a struggle (east pediment), but also the uproar as war breaks out and rages between the perpetual rivals, reason and untamed nature (west pediment).

Fully cognisant of the artistic currents of his time, the artist proceeded one stage further, opening up avenues which later generations would afterwards explore. The massive, sturdily built figures no longer stood head on and parallel to the depth of the pediment, but sideways to it, achieving three-dimensional space for the first time in large-scale sculpture. On the west pediment Deidameia (fig. p. 122) makes a spiral-like turn on her axis, which is an original contribution to the problem of three-dimensional space, and Theseus (fig. p. 123) iş presented at an angle to the depth of the pediment. On the east pediment the hindquarters of the horses of the two chariots spread sideways like a fan between the static figures of the rest of the composition which, in this position, also avoid an austere frontality. Sculptor and artist in one, the creator did not hesitate from using means directly derived from painting, wherever needed, in order to fit the mythical events into the limited space of the triangular pediment and at the same time reduce the weight of the gigantic figures on the floor. He lightened the parts of the figures which were against the tympanum and thus unseen, even hollowing the rear of the heaviest statues, wherever possible, going so far as to omit the hindquarters of the Centaurs when these were screened by other figures. He worked on his creations, correcting and altering them up until the last possible moment before they were hoisted into place.

Of course his assistants helped him in the execution of these immense and complex compositions. Indeed, the hands of other artists are obvious in the figures of the west pediment. Among those sculptures in the clearly Severe style are some exhibiting the characteristics of an older style: the conventional "archaic" expression of a Lapith (fig. p. 124), the schematised faces of the Centaurs resembling stereotyped masks (fig. pp. 122, 123, 124), the arbitrary elongation of limbs of the body (fig. p. 124) etc. By contrast, the soothsayer on the right half of the east pediment (fig. p. 115) is a most daring work, representative of the new avenues which the sculptor of the temple opened up. The clouded eyes of the seer, his wrinkled face, his body flabby with age and his shrivelled chest are elements seen for the first time in the monumental sculpture of the age.

Similar differences between the metopes of the temple are also to be noted, stamped nevertheless by the same talent and multi-faceted idiosyncracy of the artist who created the pediments.

In the overall design of the sculpted decoration of the pediment the master craftsman's assistants contributed each according to his ability; but, even taking into account the differences in execution, a unity of design is clear, just as it is obvious that one brain directed the work.

Who this brain was is as yet unknown. He is, however, the most genuine and the most brilliant representative of this cosmogonic period of Greek art.

GALLERY OF THE NIKE OF PAIONIOS

Very early in Greek art the goddess Nike personified the victorious outcome of a struggle. From the earliest times to late antiquity there are countless examples of her depiction in ancient painting, in sculpture and in small scale works.

This Nike, in Pentelic marble (height 2.11 m.), was sculpted by Paionios from Mende in Chalkidike. It stood at the southeast corner of the temple of Zeus on a triangular base, 8.81 m. high, so that the combined height of the statue and base was 10.92 m. The face, large parts of the body, chiton and himation and a large portion of the wings, as well as the wings of the eagle which she trod underfoot are missing.

The statue was a thank-offering from the Messenians and the Naupactians for their victory against the Spartans in the Archidamean war, probably in 421 B.C. The inscription reads: The Messenians and the Naupactians dedicated to Olympian Zeus a tithe of the booty taken from their enemies; a little lower down one reads: Paionios of Mende made this as well as the acroteria above the temple for which he won a prize. Here is another example of the competitive spirit and the thirst for acclaim which had permeated art and life so deeply.

This Nike, the oldest known example of monumental dimensions, marks a decisive stage in the history of Greek sculpture. While an older convention depicted her with her legs flexed, and only the wings on the shoulders and on the sandals to identify her, here, the goddess is depicted in flight, descending from Olympus to proclaim the victory of the Messenians and Naupactians over the Spartans, the best-drilled army of antiquity. Nike's headlong descent from the azure sky —the natural background

The marble statue of Nike by Paionios.

of the statue– made the thin chiton cling to her body exposing its perfect modelling, while the himation billows out in the rush of wind like the sail of a ship. The figure leans boldly forward, and the weight of the marble seems to rest on her left foot, as it stands on the plinth. Nevertheless, the stability and balance are ensured by the mass of stone at the back, though this is not apparent, since the lower part is fashioned into an eagle and much of the upper part is integrated into the folds of the himation. The eagle –whose head is easily discerned– describes a curve below the feet of the goddess, was the symbol both of Zeus and of the element air, and completes the impression that this astonishing creation is in flight. (Note the small scale plaster reconstruction of Nike).

A cube of marble three metres square was required for this truly colossal work; from this huge block the skilled craftsman was bold enough to hew this weightless figure, transforming the solidity of his material into the lightness of a puff of wind.

Half a century later, around 375 B.C. another great sculptor, probably Timotheos, was to complete the achievement with the Nike-acroteria for the temple of Asclepius at Epidaurus.

Some two hundred years later, another Nike, the Winged Victory of Samothrace, represents a further stage in the portrayal of this subject. Impressively majestic, she surges forward, no longer in flight, but set firmly amongst mortals, her foot on the prow of a ship.

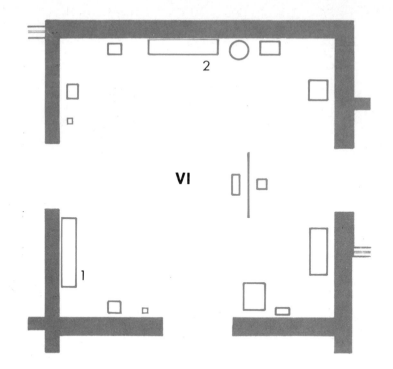

Plan of the Late Classical-Hellenistic Hall.

LATE CLASSICAL - HELLENISTIC GALLERY

As was the case with finds from the Classical era, the Sanctuary has also proved to be very poor in works from the Late Classical and Hellenistic periods. The countless statues of the gods, heroes, athletes and prominent persons which were erected in the Altis, parallel with the undiminished building activity of the day, have not survived. The few examples which do exist exhibit the change in man's spirit and in his attitude vis à vis the gods and fate (See the head of an athlete Λ99 and Praxiteles' Hermes).

Λ101. Torso with part of the legs of a child, possibly an athlete. Some believe it is a copy, others that it is an original work of the first half of the 5th century B.C.

Λ171. The lower part of a statue of Cybele seated on a throne, a lion close to her right foot. Second half of the 2nd century B.C., found in Elis.

Λ242. An unfinished statue of Nike, badly eroded. It dates from Hellenistic times and was found in Pyrgos.

Case 2

Fragments of marble statues, such as the head of Aphrodite (**Λ182**), and the upper part of a torso of Asclepius (**Λ113**), both Roman.

The little head of Aphrodite (**Λ98**) is of striking beauty with its soft folds of flesh and sweet expression. Some considet it a genuine work of Praxiteles, while others date it to the late Hellenistic period, it is of the "Knidia" type.

The head of an athlete (**Λ29**) is part of a relief as indicated by the flat back.

a

b

a) Λ98. Marble head of
Aphrodite.

b) Λ99. Marble head of an athlete.

c) Λ246. Marble portrait head of
Alexander the Great.

150

c

Details from the terracotta sima from the Leonidaion.

Of the vases, which date from the Hellenistic period, **K516** is unusual and may have had a ritual use.

On the wall

Part of a terracotta sima with lion head spouts, from the Leonidaion, the large hospice built by the Naxian architect Leonidas at his own expense in the third quarter of the 4th century B.C.

K1199. Clay jar with a lid, of the first half of the 3rd century B.C.

Λ106. Marble statue of a semi-recumbent man, perhaps Dionysos, dating from the beginning of the 4th century B.C. According to one opinion, it comes from the pediment of the Metroon.

Λ168. A half life-size marble statue of a seated woman, now headless. A bird perches on her right thigh. This is the only seated figure to have been found at Olympia out of the many fragments of Roman statuary. Below the heavy drapery folds, reminiscent of work of the Flavian period, the body still retains its supple freedom.

Right, bronze head of a child (**B2001**), dated to Hellenistic times; left, contemporary copy of the original, in tin.

Λ246. Portrait head of Alexander the Great, found at Bollantza. It is a typical depiction of the Macedonian king, with his head turned to the left, his hair like a lion's mane, his brow wrinkled, mouth half-open and gaze watery. It is probably a copy rather than an original work of the Hellenistic period.

Λ241. Statue of a lioness from Varvasaina. Her right paw rests on a ram's head. It may have been a funerary monument of the last fifteen years of the 4th century B.C.

Λ566. Corinthian half-column from the circular cella of the Philippeion, for which Philip laid the foundations after his victory at Chaironeia in 338 B.C. It was completed during the reign of Alexander the Great.

M889. Limestone base with the bronze foot of a statue. End of the 3rd century B.C.

Λ99. Marble head from the statue of a wrestler or a pancratiast, to judge of the swollen ears; the influences of the schools of Skopas and Lysippos are obvious. It dates from around 340 B.C. In this head, with its mouth still half open from the final spurt for victory and its eyes sunk deep in their sockets, the fire of classical idealism and the glowing expression of triumph are virtually extinguished. They have been replaced by a consciousness of the transience of life and the struggle for human destiny.

Λ243. Marble statue of a woman, of the Hellenistic period, found in ancient Elis.

Case 1

Statuettes of women and small heads of statuettes found in ancient Elis. Fragments of bronze statues and various vases of the Hellenistic period.

T160. Terracotta statuette of Pan, dating from 220 B.C. The goat-footed god, his genitalia emphasised, holds a crook in his right hand. Over his body is slung a panther's hide, the god retaining his primitive character as a daemon of nature.

Above Case 1

K1305. Red-figure Kalyx-krater of the 4th century B.C. probably from Elis. A couple playing a game still known today in Italy as morra can be seen; to right and left are Silenus and two female figures. On the back side are three men wrapped in their cloaks.

Part of the terracotta sima from the Leonidaion.

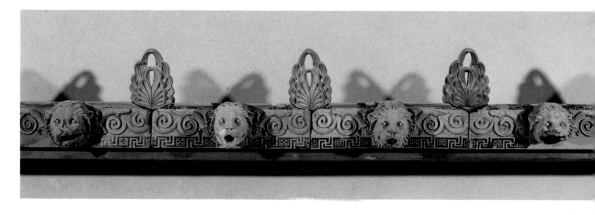

153

THE HERMES OF PRAXITELES

In his description of the sanctuary of Olympia Pausanias mentions, among the offerings at the temple of Hera, the statue of Hermes "holding the infant Dionysos" adding that it was the work of Praxiteles (Pausanias 5.17.3.). In 1877 the German excavators were fortunate enough to uncover this splendid work, which has since become one of the most famous statues of antiquity (about 330 B.C.).

The statue, 2.13 m. high, was preserved virtually undamaged, protected, until the moment of its discovery, by the fallen unbaked brick walls of the cella of the temple which was destroyed by an earthquake in the 3rd century A.D. The god, naked, holds the young Dionysos on his left arm which rests on a tree trunk over which the deep folds of his himation cascade. The new-born god impatiently stretches to grasp something which Hermes held in his right hand. It has not survived, but it may well have been a bunch of grapes, the attribute of the god of divine drunkeness, as this is known from other statues of Hermes and Dionysos and from Pompeian wall painting.

Some parts of the statue have been restored in plaster of Paris – Hermes' left leg from the knee downwards, his right calf and the lower part of the tree trunk. Hermes, the messenger of the gods, almost certainly held his metal caduceus, for the fingers of his left hand are now clenched round an empty rod-like space.

The aesthetic impact of the statue was completed by colour; traces of deep red and of gilt paint can be seen on the sandal of the surviving original foot and on the hair. Praxiteles was renowned for his blending of sculpture and paint; he even collaborated with the greatest contemporary painter, Nicias.

Toolmarks, mainly of a drove, are to be seen on part of Hermes' back, over the entire tree trunk and scouring the polish on the surface of the statue. They are commonly

The marble statue of Hermes by Praxiteles.

155

found on marble sculpture of the Roman period and have led some scholars to conclude that this is not the authentic work of Praxiteles but a later copy. However, it has escaped their notice that the tool marks both on the back and on the tree trunk, right in the angle it forms with the drapery, are at a deeper level than the carefully smoothed top surface. They must therefore be the result of a later operation on the original material, perhaps one thought necessary to remedy chance damage, possibly from an earthquake. Certainly these indications of reworking were not visible, especially those on the back, since the statue occupied one of the niches on the right-hand side of the cella, where it was found. It may be that the opportunity was taken to execute "improvements", a not infrequent occurrence in Roman times; the tree trunk was made to look more naturalistic, in keeping with the artistic taste and canons of the age. It was during this period too that two holes were drilled in the statue. Still filled with lead, one can be seen at the base of the god's spine and the other at the back of the tree trunk. They must have been made after the statue was transferred to the Heraion, in order to fasten it to the wall of the temple and thus secure it from being damaged by future earthquakes.

Inspection of the pedestal leads us to the same conclusion; its base and its capital are of different stone. While the base and trunk are the 4th century original, the Neo-Attic Kymation of the anta-capital shows that it belongs to a later date.

The pronounced polishing of the "skin" of the statue, which made many scholars uneasy, is a finish not unknown in sculpture of the 4th century B.C. Rather the contrary: it is perhaps one of the most typical stylistic traits of Praxiteles who was apparently famed for it. Ancient sources repeatedly comment on the polishing which was the hallmark of his works; even though many of the authors lived much later (for example, Quintilian, Ausonius and Amianus Marcellinus), their information is valuable.

The Hermes is a very real reflection of the spirit and tendencies of the 4th century B.C. This century, fundamentally different from the 5th, was troubled by social and economic problems as well as by philosophical and religious disquiet. The Greeks of the late Classical period brooded over the certainty and strength of their forebears which had been lost forever; exhausted, they sought the serenity and relaxation enjoyed by the gods in the Elysian fields. The artists who had inherited the firm-rooted tradition and rich experiences of the achievements of the 5th century B.C. moved on to find new outlets for artistic expression. Realism and naturalism, which had already made their appearance, in early Classical times, though only fitfully are now found fully developed.

Mortals were no longer depicted idealistically, but increasingly "in actual time and space" – in their daily occupations and in a three-dimensional setting. The gods, on the other hand, were portrayed in Olympian calm and beatitude, as described in Homeric epic, far removed from good and evil, far from the fickleness of fortune and from the wretchedness of the human condition. They were no longer shown in action as they had been in the 5th century B.C., but seated or standing, leaning nonchalantly against a support of some kind.

In this statue even Hermes is supported against a tree trunk as he stopped to take a brief rest during his journey with the new-born Dionysos to his nurses at Nysa in Boeotia. He seems to amuse the immortal child, though the gaze of his melancholy, pensive eyes is lost in contemplation of the unknown.

His lithe body, pulsing with life even when standing still, emphasises the rooted immobility of the tree which here is not just a prop as it later became, especially in Roman works, but an integral part of the composition. The well-proportioned, well-built athletic body, in clear contrast with the delicate translucent highly polished surface of the skin, here becomes more ethereal, befitting divinity. Finally, the arrangement of the limbs and muscles from top to bottom of the body in positions variously of rest and of motion or of support against the tree endow the statue with a balanced relaxation which only sculptors of the 4th century B.C., and Praxiteles in particular, managed to convey. The statue is permeated not by the symmetry of the 5th century, but by the balanced rhythm, the eurythmy, which is one of the most distinctive features of art in the later Classical period.

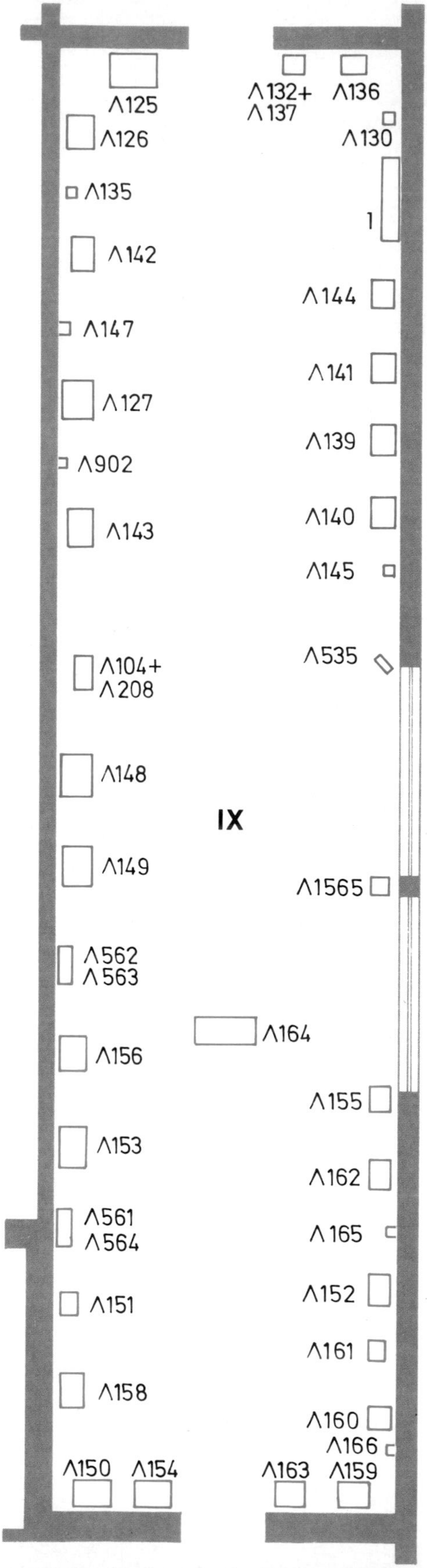

∧125
∧126
∧135
∧142
∧147
∧127
∧902
∧143
∧104+
∧208
∧148
∧149
∧562
∧563
∧156
∧153
∧561
∧564
∧151
∧158
∧150   ∧154

∧132+
∧137   ∧136
∧130

1

∧144
∧141
∧139
∧140
∧145
∧535

IX

∧1565

∧164
∧155
∧162
∧165
∧152
∧161
∧160
∧166
∧163   ∧159

Plan of the Roman Hall.

ROMAN HALL

Roman art in Greece and in the eastern provinces in general developed differently from art in the capital. Though formalisation and rigidity remained a common factor, Greek artists, guided by the dictates of Rome, confined standardisation to subject matter, enriching it with the freshness of the Greek spirit and with purely Greek quirks of expression. Insctiptions preserved on statue bases of the period at Olympia show that the artisans were Greeks and indeed often Athenians (see **Λ125, Λ140, Λ141, Λ143**).

Λ132 + Λ137. Statue of a man, in heroic guise, perhaps contemporary with **Λ130** (see below), with the typical hairstyle and watery gaze characteristic of the Julio-Claudian era. It is a copy of a 4th century B.C. original in the style of the "Richelieu" Hermes in the Louvre.

Λ136. Torso of a statue in Pentelic marble. First century B.C., copy of the famous "spearbearer", the work of the Argive sculptor Polykleitos (450-420 B.C.).

Λ130. This head, perhaps a portrait of Nero Drusus, or rather Tiberius Gemellus, is typical of the latter part of the Julio-Claudian era. Its mild, dreamy sunken eyes are a characteristic trait of that era.

Case 1

Pottery for everyday use, undecorated. The most interesting, though poorly executed, of the figurines are **Π2942** which depicts an inebriated old man, a cup in his right hand, and **T159** and **T350** which belong to the "grylloi" type. This nomenclature denotes one variation on a type of badly made caricature dwarfs with large head and hump which ridiculed the public figures of the time. According to Pliny they were first devised in the late 4th

a

160

b

a) Λ132+Λ137. Marble statue of an heroicized man in the type of the "Richelieu" Hermes.

b) Λ144. Marble statue of a woman, known as Poppea Sabina.

161

century B.C. to mock the painter Antiphilos, but the type is in fact far older; it first appears on late Archaic painted vases.

T159. From an unknown atelier, must have been made around the middle of the 1st century B.C., while **T350,** from an Alexandrine workshop, dates from the second half of the 3rd century B.C.

The four statues which follow were all found in the Heraion:

Λ144. Formerly, scholars were of the opinion that this statue depicted Poppaea Sabina, the wife of Nero. A more recent theory, however, regards it as the portrait of some noble woman of Elis, shown as a priestess, perhaps of Hera since it was found in her temple.

Three headless statues of Elean women of aristocratic birth, dated from the 2nd half of the 1st century A.D.

Λ141. The inscription on the plinth tells us that this was the work of the Athenian Eleusineios.

Λ139. This statue, in the style of the tall woman from Herculaneum in the Albertinum Museum, Dresden, is the work of the Athenian Aulus Sextus Eraton, as the inscription carved on the right knee tells us.

Λ140. According to an inscription on a fold of drapery above the left knee, this is the work of the Athenian sculptor, Eros.

Λ145. Portrait head of a woman of aristocratic lineage, dating from the second half of the 1st century A.D.

Λ535. The list of names of the staff of the sanctuary of Olympia between the 188th and 189th Olympiad (28-24 B.C.), carved on marble tile from the temple of Zeus. It has been made to look like a stele with a pediment and antefixes.

Five statues in this hall – Claudius, Titus, Domitian (?) or perhaps Vespasian, Agrippina the younger(?) and the so-called Domitia – were found in the Metroon. This temple was converted first into a cult centre of Augustus and later into a shrine to all the Roman emperors.

Λ125. The statue of the emperor Claudius (A.D. 41-54) is the best preserved of those found in the Metroon. The melancholy, introspective eyes are in strong contrast to the proud, triumphant stance which imitates the typical depiction of Zeus. His left hand would have rested on a sceptre while the right hand held a Nike or an orb, or possibly both. At his feet is an eagle. The inscription reads: *Philathenaios and Hegias, Athenians, made this.* The date of the statue is a matter of debate. Some believe that it belongs to the middle of the century, others that it

Λ535. Marble tile from the temple of Zeus with a list of the names of the temple staff.

163

a

164

b

a) Λ125. Marble statue of the emperor Claudius.

b) Λ143. Marble statue of a woman, known as Agrippina the Younger.

is later, dating from the Flavian period, but based on Claudian originals.

Λ126. Statue of the emperor Titus (A.D. 79-81) as a general. He wears on oak wreath and his eyes look upwards in the style of the Hellenistic "apotheosis". A relief gorgoneion, Nereids on sea-horses and dolphins decorate the breastplate, while the head of Ammon, an eagle etc., in relief, adorn the strips. His sword rests on a tree trunk close to his right foot. The work may have originated in a Roman atelier; the characteristics of Flavian art are pronounced, in the massive clumsy head and flabby flesh.

Λ135. Portrait head of a bald man, perhaps a priest, 3rd century A.D. Recent opinion regards this head as belonging to a statue in the Nymphaion, probably that of M. Appius Bradua, grandfather of Regilla (see below). It has been dated to the 2nd century A.D.

Λ142. Headless statue of a woman. Though it had been thought that it depicted the empress Domitia, wife of Domitian (A.D. 81-96), this theory has recently been revised. The thick, almost heavy folds of the clothing do not conceal the desire to reveal the body, which indeed betrays a Greek artistic trait.

Λ147. Portrait head of a woman wearing a diadem, probably a member of the imperial family. It may date to the time of Claudius.

Λ127. Headless statue of a Roman emperor as a general, believed by some to be Domitian and by others to be Vespasian. The corselet bears, in relief, a gorgoneion, two victories erecting a trophy with a seated male figure on its base. On the strips of the corselet are the usual reliefs: gorgoneion, eagle etc. Close to the right foot is a kneeling hostage. The depiction of Roman emperors as generals is frequently found in the later Julio-Claudian era, though they are also often portrayed as gods or heroes or even in civilian dress.

Λ902. Portrait head of a woman with rather artificially dressed hair. Late 2nd century A.D.

Λ134. Statue of a woman, probably Agrippina the Younger (A.D. 15-59), wife of Claudius and mother of Nero. The himation covers the head, and indicates her portrayal as a priestess. It is one of the most beautiful Roman statues to have been found in the sanctuary. On the plinth is the inscription: *Dionysios Apollonios of Athens made this.* The date of this statue is debated, some ascribing it to the Claudian, others to the Flavian period (see above **Λ125**)

Λ104 + Λ208. Statue of an athlete, endowed with the characteristics of Antinous and possibly even Antinous himself – the youthful favourite of the emperor Hadrian

Λ104+Λ208. Detail from the marble statue of an athlete or possibly of Antinous.

(A.D. 117-138). It is one of the many statues commissioned by the emperor after the young man's premature death. The Classical ideals, now dessicated, to which the taste of the age was returning, show through the beautiful features of the dreamily expressive face.

Most of the statues in this Gallery stood in the Nymphaion, a monumental fountain, and an example of Roman imperial architecture. It was the offering of Herodes Atticus and his wife Regilla, priestess of Demeter Chamyne. The building dates from around A.D. 160. Studiedly sumptuous and alien to its setting in the sanctuary, it was the last magnificent building to be erected in the Altis. According to a recent theory, the statues stood in the eleven niches on either floor of the two-storeyed building. The statues on the lower storey, dedicated by Herodes, depicted members of the imperial house of the Antonines; those on the upper storey, offered by the Eleans, represented members of the donor's family. Most of the Nymphaion statues have been identified tentatively with particular personages. The criteria used are the known iconic characteristics of each statue coupled with the inscriptions on the bases which were found within the building and preserve the names of the figures.

Λ148. Statue of the emperor Hadrian (A.D. 117-138) wearing a laurel wreath. His left hand once held a spear. The immobility of the figure, despite the fact that one foot is placed in front of the other, and the rigidity of the modelling are typical. On the cuirass two relief Nikes crown a palladium; to right and left are a snake and an owl. The palladium is above the wolf who suckled Romulus and Remus seated on a sprouting calyx. The association of these pictorial attributes echoes the Greco-Roman education of the philhellene emperor.

Λ149. Headless statue of an emperor; according to some it is Trajan (A.D. 97-117), according to others Marcus Aurelius (A.D. 161-180), clad as a general. He too would have grasped a spear in his left hand. On his cuirass, above plant decoration, are relief griffins, separated by a lamp-stand. The strips of the cuirass would have been painted and the sandals made of panther skin. A palm tree, leafed and in fruit, rests against the statue close to the right foot. Very academic piece of work, with a metallic hardness in the rendering of the drapery, it has recently been maintained that it belongs to a later phase of the decoration of the Nymphaion, like the toga-clad statue, **Λ154.**

Λ563, Λ562 and beyond them **Λ561, Λ564.** Corinthian anta capitals from the Nymphaion.

Λ156. Headless statue of a woman in the style of the

tall woman from Herculaneum. According to some, it portays the wife of Herodes Atticus, Regilla; others believe it to be her mother. The head of this quality work was an integral part of the statue, not inserted as is usual in most statues from the Nymphaion.

Λ153. Headless statue of a Roman wearing a toga, with a scrinium (a chest with a lock) at his left foot; it is probably Appius Annius Gallus, the father of Regilla.

Λ151. Headless statue of a boy. It may perhaps depict Regillus the Younger, son of Herodes Atticus and Regilla. There is a small scrinium close to his left foot. The statue originally stood on the same base as that of his sister Athenais.

Λ158. Headless statue of a woman, possibly Elpinike, elder daughter of Herodes Atticus, or Faustina the Younger, the wife of Marcus Aurelius.

Λ150. Headless statue of a Roman emperor dressed as a general, possibly Marcus Aurelius (A.D. 161-180), but executed before he ascended to the purple, since the statue is small in relation to the others. A relief gorgoneion decorates the cuirass; close to his right foot is a palm tree with leaves and fruit.

Λ154. Headless statue of a Roman wearing a toga, possibly Herodes Atticus himself (A.D. 101-177). Close to his left foot stands a scrinium. It has recently been maintained that like the statue **Λ149** this too belongs to a later phase of the decoration of the Nymphaion.

Λ163. Headless statue of a woman holding a libation phial. It is probably Regilla, wife of Herodes Atticus, or, according to a more recent opinion, his daughter Elpinike.

Λ159. Statue in the style of the small woman from Herculaneum (a statue from ancient Herculaneum, now in Dresden). Some think it depicts Faustina the Younger, wife of the emperor Marcus Aurelius, others Athenais, second daughter of Herodes Atticus. Despite the freshness and tenderness of the expression an icy immobility stamps the features (see **Λ160**).

Λ166. Portrait head of Lucius Verus (A.D. 161-169) at a young age. He wears a crown of laurel, with a medallion in the centre. His sword-arm is also preserved, as well as a fragment of his cuirass, so he must have been depicted in military dress. The name Verus which was added to his first name after his proclamation as an emperor, appears in the inscription on the base.

Λ160. Statue of a girl. Probably one of the daughters of Marcus Aurelius and Faustina the Younger, either Annia Galeria Faustina or Lucilla. The inscription tells us that

a

b

*a) Λ166. Marble portrait head of
Lucius Verus.*

*b) Λ165. Marble portrait head of
Antoninus Pius.*

170

the statue of the girl stood on the same base as that of her brother, T. Aelius Antoninus.

Λ161. Headless statue of Athenais, younger daughter of Herodes Atticus. According to the inscription, it shared a base with the statue of her brother, Regillus.

Λ152. This headless statue depicted either M. Atilius Atticus, the elder son of Herodes, or his son-in-law, L. Vibullius Hipparchus. More recent opinion postulates that it could also have portrayed T. Claudius Atticus Herodes, father of the donor. In his right hand he held a bowl, a common symbol of veneration.

Λ165. Portrait head of the Emperor Antoninus Pius (A.D. 138-161) from his statue in the Nymphaion. A laurel wreath crowns his hair and the medallion on his forehead bears the insignia of an eagle in relief.

Λ162. Headless statue of a woman, probably Athenais, grand-daughter of Herodes Atticus and daughter of L. Vibullius Hipparchus; or it might be A. Kaukidia Tertulla, Regilla's mother.

Λ155. The upper part of a statue of Faustina the Elder, wife of Antoninus Pius. Like **Λ156** it is in the style of the tall woman from Herculaneum, but its execution is inferior.

Λ164. This statue of a bull was erected as a symbol of the element of water and stood above the lower pool of the Nymphaion (see the reconstruction drawing). The inscription on the bull tells us that the entire structure was the offering of Regilla to Zeus.

Λ1565. Corinthian capital from the Nymphaion.

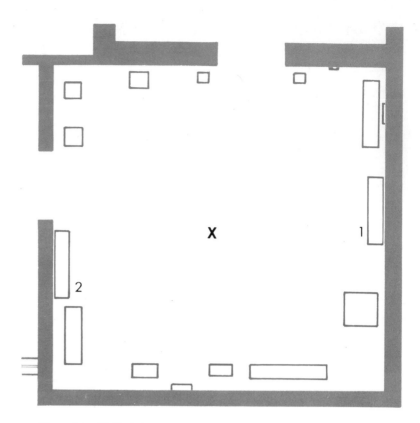

Plan of the Hall of the Olympic Games.

GALLERY OF THE OLYMPIC GAMES

Λ111, Λ112. Two small headless Pentelic marble statues of Nemesis-Tyche. The goddess holds her attributes, a measure and a rudder balanced on a wheel. The statues originally stood to the right and left of the "Krypte", as the entrance to the stadium of the second century A.D. was called.

EM6462. Cast of an inscribed bronze plaque from Olympia now in the National Archaeological Museum of Athens. In the Elean dialect it records an honorary decree voted by the Eleans in favour of Democrates of Tenedos, son of Aletor. On the pediment are the emblems of Tenedos, a bunch of grapes and double axe. 3rd c. A.D.

Λ412. Marble gravestone of Camillus from Alexandria, dating from the 3rd century A.D. The inscription reads: *Agathos daimon Camelos of Alexandria, boxer, winner in the Nemean Games, died here in the stadium while he was boxing after he prayed to Zeus to give him either the crown or death. He was 35 years old. Farewell.* It was found at Frangonisi to the east of the sanctuary and had probably been taken there from Olympia. Even at that late date, the splendour of the Games was still untarnished.

Two shelly limestone blocks, pieces from the starting line of the early Classical stadium.

Case 1

Top shelf: The statuettes **B2400, B26** and **B6767 + 7500** merit attention. The statuette of the young man **B2400** follows the style of the kouros. The crown of pointed leaves (? palm leaves) may represent the Thyreatic crown worn by the leaders of the chorus of the children at Sparta, participants in an annual festival held to commemorate the Spartan victory over the Argives at Thyrea. It is from a Laconian workshop, dating immediately after the middle of the 6th century B.C.

B26 is the statuette of a runner in the starting position, an offering to Zeus from an Olympic victor. It was made in an Argive atelier around 490 B.C. The inscription on the left thigh reads: *I belong to Zeus.* The statuette **B6767** depicts a discus-thrower at the moment his body turns backwards before releasing the discus which he holds in

M348, M349, M281. Bronze strigils.

his raised hands. Together with the runner **B26** and three other statuettes – of a jumper, a javelin-thrower and a wrestler– it seems to form a group and could be the offering of a victor in the pentathlon. On the left side is the inscription: *I belong to Zeus.* Argive work of around 490 B.C.

The bronze Elean coin **M876**, from the reign of Hadrian is interesting because its reverse shows the silver and ivory table on which the crowns of the Olympic victors were placed; it was a 5th century B.C. work by the sculptor Kolotis.

Middle shelf: Strigils, **M348, M349** of bronze and **M229** and **M227** of iron; these were used by athletes to cleanse their bodies of the oil they used during training and of the sand which helped remove the oil. Bronze discoi.

Bottom shelf: Stone jumping weights and a bronze discus, **M891**, the offering of Poplius Asklepiades, a victor in the pentathlon. It is inscribed on both sides: a) *Thank-offering to Olympian Zeus* [from] *Poplius Asklepiades of Corinth, victor in the pentathlon in the 255th Olympiad* and b) the confirmation of the officer to whom the offering was delivered; not to be outshone, he discloses, proudly his own pretensions to grandeur to the passer by: *To Olympian Zeus* [received] *by Alytarches* (chief of police) *Flavius Scribonianus, the relative of senators and consuls, 456th Olympiad.* The date given in the first inscription, the 255th Olympiad, is 241 A.D., while the second gives the 456th Olympiad. The discrepancy is not due to a mistake but to a different way of rectioning the Olympiads, in the second instance based not on the usual 776 but on 1580 as the starting date. This latter inscription is typical of the contemporary tendency to seek a kernel of historic truth in early myths and a fascination with the distant past, when the Games were established.

Λ45. Badly damaged statue base of the victorious Olympic pancratiast Polydamas. So great was the fame of his achievements that the king of the Persians Darius II, Ochos, invited him to Susa. There he was challenged to a duel with three combatants at once, formidable infantrymen from the ranks of the invincibles, and won. On the front of the base, Darius and four women watch Polydamas in astonishment. He has lifted his opponent into the air. On the narrow sides, the athlete is shown: a) wrestling with a lion, like a latter-day Herakles, b) seated on the defeated beast. A work of the second half of the 4th century from the atelier of the great Sicyonian sculptor Lysippos.

Λ570. Base of a votive in the form of an Ionic capital,

B26. Bronze statuette of an athlete.

a

M876. Bronze Elean coin.

b

a) B2400. Bronze statuette of a youth.

b) B3005. Bronze figurine of a charioteer in his chariot.

4th century B.C.

Λ536. Pentelic marble base of a votive, reminiscent of a doric column capital. On it stood the statue of the Elean Charops, a victor in the equestrian events. On the front side of the abacus is the inscription: *Charops of Elis, son of Telemachus, victor in the horse race.* It dates from the 1st century B.C.

Λ537. The upper part of a Roman statue base in Pentelic marble. The front side bears the inscription: *Theoxena, (daughter of) Telestas [dedicated] to Olympian Zeus the statue of Alkeias the herald, her son from Damaretos.*

Λ191. A sandstone weight, inscribed with the proud boast that the athlete Bybon lifted it above his head with one hand: *Bybon, son of Phola, lifted me over his head with one hand.* The stone weights 143.5 kilos. End of the 7th or beginning of the 6th century B.C.

Wall Case

Λ189, Λ190b. Stone jumping-weights used by competitors in the long jump which formed part of the pentathlon (see the painting on a vase in the National Archaeological Museum of Athens). The inscription on **Λ189**, which dates from the late 6th or early 5th century B.C. reads: *Akmatidas the Spartan dedicated this when he was victorious, without touching the dust of the arena* (i.e. without having to set foot in the stadium). In other words he was judged against another competitor, either because the other did not present himself, or, exhausted by another event, he conceded to the superiority of Akmatidas without a contest.

Λ42. Base of a statue in the shape of an astragal (an ankle bone), made of Laconian marble and dating from the 5th century B.C. An astragal symbolized good luck, chiefly in athletic events.

Λ532. Base for a statue of the Elean Pythocles, Victor in the *pentathlon* on 452 B.C. Two inscriptions are preserved; the older gives us the manes of the champion Pythocles and of the sculptor Polycleitos (it is uncertain whether it refers to the older or the younger). The newer inscription: (Dedicated by) *Pythocles the Eleian, made by Polycleitos the Argive*, probably of the first century either B.C. or A.D. will have been carved with a clear effort to imitate the older letters ehen the statue was replaced, either because of weathering, or because the original was plundered orfor some other reason.

Λ529. Part of the black limestome circular base of the statue of Kyniska, sister of Agesilaos (398-358 B.C.), king

TC1958. Terracotta figurine of a charioteer.

of Sparta. Kyniska boasts that she is the daughter and sister of kings as well as the only woman in Greece to be an Olympic winner. Most of the four line inscription has survived: *Kings of Sparta were my forefathers and my brothers, Victorious Kyniska with her chariot* [drawn by] *swift-footed horses erected this statue. I assert that I am the only woman in all Greece who has won this crown. Made by Apelleas son of Kallikles* (390-380 B.C.).

Case 2

This case houses a display of pottery or bronze objects associated with the equestrian events or chariot races of the Geometric and Archaic periods. On the top shelf are the horses **B1301**, the riders **Π2946**, the charioteers **Π2929**, and **B777** and on the middle shelf, the charioteer **Π2935** and horse's head **T8270**. The chariots of the charioteers **TC1958** and **B3005** on the top shelf have also survived. There are wheels **Π2928** and **T8330** on the top shelf, and chariots **TC606** and **B1389** are to be seen on the middle shelf. Finally, on the bottom shelf are reins, for example **B1460.**

The fragment from the leg of a tripod **B1665**, dated to 760 B.C., is interesting. It shows a man standing on the back of a horse. The raised arms suggests that he may be a god, a motif borrowed from New Hittite art.

Λ531. The black limestone base of a statue of the boxer Aristion of Epidauros. The inscription: (dedicated by) *Aristion, son of Theophiles of Epidauros, made by Polycleitos,* dates from the middle of the 4th century B.C. The statue would certainly have been the work of Polycleitos the Younger, the peak of whose activity falls in the first half of the 4th century B.C.

Λ530. Base of a statue of Xenocles from Mainalos, winner of the children's wrestling. The names of the victor, *Xenocles* [son of]*Euthyphron* [from] *Mainalos,* and of the sculptor, *Polycleitos,* are recorded on the upper face of the base which is of Peloponnesian marble. The inscription on the front of the base reads: *Xenocles son of Euthyphron from Mainalos who was victorious in wrestling over four competitors without falling,* probably means that Xenocles beat four contestants in wrestling only, but not in boxing. It is not known whether the older or the younger Polycleitos is referred to.

Λ192. Marble chair belonging to the Spartan Gorgos, consul of the Eleians, inscribed: *Gorgos the Lacedaemonian proxenos of the Eleians.* It dates from the second half of the 6th or the beginning of the 5th century B.C.

BIBLIOGRAPHY

ANCIENT LITERARY SOURCES

FRAZER, J.G., *Pausanias' Description of Greece* [with an English translation and a commentary] vols 6. London 1898-1913.

FRAZER, J.G., BUREN, A.W. van, *Graecia antiqua*. Maps and plans to illustrate Pausanias' Description of ancient Greece. London 1930.

JONES, W.H.S., *Pausanias' Description of Greece* [with an English translation in 4 vols, and with a companion volume containing maps, plans and indices]. London 1965-1971.

MEYER, E., *Pausanias' Beschreibung Griechenlands* [Neu übersetzt, mit einer Einleitung und erklärenden Ammerkungen] (Zürich, Stuttgart, 1967^2) pp. 605 ff.

XENOPHON, *Hellenica*, 7, 4, 14, 28-32.

ΠΑΠΑΧΑΤΖΗΣ, Ν., *Παυσανίου Ελλάδος Περιήγησις*. Βιβλία 5ο και 6ο [Αρχαίο κείμενο, μετάφραση και σημειώσεις ιστορικές, αρχαιολογικές και μυθολογικές]. Athens 1979.

PAUSANIAS, *Description of Greece*, Book 5th and 6th.

POLYBIUS, *The Histories*, 4, 73 ff. and passim.

STRABO, *Geographica*, 8, 30 pp. 350-355.

GUIDE BOOKS

KIRSTEN, E.,-KRAIKER, *Griechenlandkunde*, 2 vols. Heidelberg 1967^2. 265 ff.

ROSSITER, S., *Blue Guide*. London 1986.

YALOURIS, N., *Olympia. Altis and Museum*. Munich 1983^2. [Also in French and German].

GENERAL - HISTORY

BERVE, H. et al. *Griechische Tempel und Heiligtümer*. München 1961. 10 ff., 118 ff.

BLOUET, A., *Expédition Scientifique de Morée* I. Paris 1831-1838. 56 ff.

BÖTTICHER, A., *Olympia.* Berlin 1883 (rev. 1886[2]).

CURTIUS, E., *Olympia.* Berlin 1935.

CURTIUS, E., ADLER, F., *Olympia, Die Ergebnisse*, 5 vols. Berlin 1966[2].

Deutsches Archäologisches Institut. *Berichte über die Ausgrabungen in Olympia*, 10 vols (1937-1976), continuing.

Deutsches Archäologisches Institut: *Olympische Forschungen*, 16 vols (1944-1984), continuing.

DÖRPFELD, W., *Alt-Olympia.* Berlin 1966[2].

DREES, L., *Olympia.* New York 1968.

GARDINER, N.E., *Olympia, its history and remains.* Oxford 1925.

HERRMANN, H.V., *Zur ältesten Geschichte von Olympia:* Athenische Mitteilungen 77 (1962) 3 ff.

HERRMANN, H.V., *Olympia, Heiligtum und Wettkampfstätte.* München 1972.

HOENLE, A., *Olympia in der Politik der griechischen Staatenwelt.* Tübingen 1968.

JANTZEN, U., *Enciclopedia dell' Arte Antica* V (1963) 635 ff. s.v. Olympia.

KONTHΣ, I., *Το ιερόν της Ολυμπίας κατά τον Δ΄ αιώνα π.X.,* Athens 1958.

KUNZE, E., Olympia: *Neue Deutsche Ausgrabungen im Mittelmeergebiet und im Vorderasien.* Berlin 1959. 263 ff.

ΛΕΟΝΑΡΔΟΣ, B., *Ολυμπία.* Athens 1901.

MEYER, E., *Der kleine Pauly* 4 (1972) 279 ff. s.v. Olympia.

WIESNER, J., *Pauly-Wissowa* XVIII (1939) 1 ff. s.v. Olympia.

YALOURIS, N., *The Princeton Encyclopedia of Classical sites.* Princeton 1976. 640 ff. s.v. Olympia.

ZIEHEN, L., *Pauly-Wissowa* XVII 2 (1937) 2520 ff. s.v. Olympia.

GAMES - CULT

BENGTSON, H., *Die Olympischen Spiele in der Antike.* Zürich 1971.

BILINSKI, B., *Agoni Ginnici*: Accademia Polaca Delle Scienze. Biblioteca e Centro di Studi a Roma (Warszava 1979). Nr. 75.

DEUBNER, L., *Kult und Spiele im alten Olympia.* Leipzig 1936.

FURTWÄNGLER, A., *Die Bedeutung der Gymnastik in der griechischen-Kunst*: "Der Säemann" Monatschrift für pädagogischen Reform. Leipzig-Berlin 1905. 4 ff.

GARDINER, N.E., *Athletics of the Ancient World.* Oxford 1930.

GLUBOK, SH., TAMARIN, A., *Olympic Games in Ancient Greece.* London 1976.

HARRIS, H.A., *Greek Athletes and Athletics.* London 1972.

—, *Sport in Greece and Rom*. London 1972.

JÜTHNER, J., *Die athletischen Leibesübungen der Griechen* τόμοι 2. Wien 1965-1968.

—, *Herkunft und Grundlagen der Griechischen Nationalspiele:* Die Antike 15, 1939, 231 ff.

MEULI, K., *Der Ursprung der Olympischen Spiele:* Die Antike: 17 (1941) 189 ff.

MEZÖ, F., *Geschichte der Olympischen Spiele*. München 1930.

MILLER, S.G., ARETE. Chicago 1979.

—, *The date of the Olympic Festivals:* Athenische Mitteilungen 90 (1975) 215 ff.

MORETTI, L., *Olympionikai, vincitori negli antichi agoni:* Mem. Linc. ser. 8, 8, 2 (1957) 53 κ.ε.

—, *Supplemente al Katalogo degli Olympionikai:* Klio 52 (1970). 295 ff.

OLIVOVA, VERA, *Sport und Spiel im Altertum*. München 1985.

RUDOLF, W., *Olympischer Kampfsport in der Antike*. Berlin 1965.

SPIESER, J.M., *La christianisation des sanctuaires païens en Grèce:* Deutsches Archäologisches Institut, Abteilung Athen: Neue Forschungen in Griechischen Heiligtümern. Tübingen 1976. 309 ff.

SWANDLING, J., *The Ancient Olympic Games*. London 1980.

ARCHITECTURE

GRUBEN, G., *Die Tempel der Griechen*. München 1976². 43 ff.

GRUNAUER, P., *Der Westgiebel des Zeustempels von Olympia:* Jahrbuch des Deutschen Archäologischen Instituts 89 (1974) 1 ff.

—, *Der Zeustempel in Olympia:* Bonner Jahrbücher 171 (1971) 114 ff.

—, *Der Zeustempel in Olympia:* Berichte der Koldewey-Gesellschaft 25 (1969) 13 ff.

HERRMANN, K., *Die Giebelrekonstruktion des Schatzhauses von Megara:* Athenische Mitteilungen 89 (1974) 75 ff.

—, *Beobachtungen zur Schatzhaus-Architektur Olympias:* Deutsches Archäologisches Institut. Abteilung Athen: Neue Forschungen in Griechischen Heiligtümern (Tübingen) 1976, 321 ff.

HÖPFNER, W., *Zwei Ptolemäerbauten:* Athenische Mitteilungen. Suppl. 1 (1971).

MALLWITZ, A., *Neue Forschungen in Olympia:* Epeteris tes Hetaireias Eliakon Meleton vol. 1 1982, 436-462.

—, *Olympia und seine Bauten*. München 1972.

MIŁLER, S., *The Prytaneion at Olympia*: Athenische Mitteilungen 86 (1971) 79 ff.

SMITH, J.R., *The Temple of Zeus at Olympia*: Memoirs of the American Academy 4, 1924, 153 ff.

YALOURIS, N., Das Akroter des Heraions in Olympia: Athenische Mitteilungen 87 (1972) 85 ff.

ART

ASHMOLE, B., *Architect and Sculptor in Classical Greece*. London 1972. pp. 1-89.

ASHMOLE, B., YALOURIS N., *The Sculptures of the temple of Zeus*. London 1967.

BECATTI, G., *Problemi Fidiaci*. Milano 1951.

—, *Controversie Olympiche*, Studi Miscellanei 18 (1971) 67 ff.

BLÜMEL, C., *Der Hermes eines Praxiteles*. Baden-Baden 1948.

BUSCHOR, E., *Die Olympiameister*: Athenische Mitteilungen 51 (1926) 163 ff.

BUSCHOR, E., HAMANN R., *Die Skulpturen des Zeustempels zu Olympia*. Marburg 1924.

ECKSTEIN, F., *Αναθήματα*. Berlin 1969.

FINK, J., *Der Thron des Zeus in Olympia*. München 1967.

HEGE, W., RODENWALDT, G., *Olympia*. Berlin 1936.

HEILMEYER, W., *Giessereibetriebe in Olympia*, Jahrbuch des Deutschen Archäologischen Instituts 84 (1969) 1 ff.

HYDE, W.W., *Olympic victor monuments and Greek athletic art*. Washington 1921.

KRAAY, C.M., *Greek Coins*. New York 1966.

KREUZER, A., *Des Praxiteles Hermes von Olympia*. Berlin 1948.

LIEGLE, J., *Der Zeus des Phidias*. Berlin 1952.

MALLWITZ, A., HERRMANN, H.V., *Die Funde aus Olympia*. Athen 1980.

RICHTER, G., *The Pheidian Zeus at Olympia*: Hesperia 35 (1966) 166 ff.

RIDGWAY, B., *The Severe Style in Greek Sculpture*. Princeton 1970.

SÄFLUND, M.L., *The East Pediment of the temple of Zeus at Olympia*. Göteborg 1970.

SELTMANN, C., *The temple coins of Olympia*. Cambridge 1921.

SIMON, E., *Zu den Giebeln des Zeustempels von Olympia*: Athenische Mitteilungen 83 (1968) 147 ff.